D1830818

AN UNFREQUENTED HIGHWAY THROUGH SIKKIM AND TIBET TO CHUMOLAORI

AN UNFREQUENTED HIGHWAY THROUGH SIKKIM AND TIBET TO CHUMOLAORI

JOHN EASTON

SIXTEEN PLATES

Published by

GYAN

Gyan Publishing House
5, Ansari Road
Daryaganj, New Delhi-110002
Phone: 011-47034999, 9811692060
E-mail: books@gyanbooks.com

Distribution Network
gyanbooks.com
India, USA, Canada, UK, Australia, France

© Publisher

All rights reserved. No part of this work may be reproduced, stored, adapted, or transmitted in any form or by any means, electronic, mechanical, photocopying, micro-filming, recording or otherwise, or translated in any language, without the prior written permission of the copyright owner and the publisher.

ISBN : 978-81-212-4179-3 (PB)
First Published, London, 1928

2nd Impression 2020

Printed at: Gyan Press, Delhi.

The book is sold subject to the condition that it shall not, by way of trade or otherwise, be lent, resold, hired out, or otherwise circulated without the prior publisher's written consent.

**An
Unfrequented Highway through
Sikkim and Tibet to Chumolaori**
Author: John Easton

AN UNFREQUENTED HIGHWAY

THROUGH SIKKIM AND TIBET

TO CHUMOLAORI

BY

JOHN EASTON

LONDON

THE SCHOLARTIS PRESS: 30 MUSEUM STREET

1928

PHARI

'Beyond the fortress, rising straight from the plain, lay the snow-white mountain Chumolaori.'

CONTENTS

CONTENTS

FOREWORD

PHARI, as the crow flies, is approximately four hundred and fifty miles from Calcutta, and two-thirds of that distance is traversed by the Eastern Bengal Railway: a train journey of twelve hours divided into two sections. The first section of railroad is standard gauge: it terminates at Santahar, where the traveller changes into a narrow-gauge section and proceeds to the terminus at Siliguri, lying at the base of the Himalayan foothills. The journey through the plains of Bengal has been hot, dirty and tedious: the scenery monotonous: unbroken plains of cultivated land and paddy fields, with an occasional mud village or group of farms: colourless save when the sun rises or sets: telling no tale except at Paksey, where the Ganges sweeps on its turbulent course.

At Siliguri the country puts on a new face. Close wooded foothills loom up ahead: a cool breeze from the snows spells relief in store for the jaded European; squat Mongol types from the neighbouring hills banish memories of the *dhoti* and the spectacled babu. Here the miniature railway in two long tracks sets out on its climb. The western track climbs to Darjeeling, the summer capital of Bengal: the eastern winds up the Teesta valley to Kalimpong in British Bhutan.

Darjeeling and British Bhutan are districts of Bengal. They lie side by side and together comprise a strip of territory fifty miles broad and twenty miles deep snatched from the state of Sikkim to afford a haven for wearied officials and a prosperous corner for the tea-planting community. They are bounded on the west by Nepal and on the east by Bhutan, two independent states, both sacrosanct and closed to the wandering traveller. Northward lies Sikkim, a British Indian state ruled by a Maharajah, stretching as far as the Great Himalayan range and the Tibetan passes.

From Kalimpong the road climbs north-east through Sikkim for fifty miles to the Tibetan passes of the Donkhia range, where one crosses the frontier; thence it descends into the Chumbi valley, and continues north-eastwards a further fifty miles to the Tableland of Tibet. It is the hundred miles of road from Kalimpong to Phari that this book sets forth to describe.

To the men and beasts who were the companions of my journey tribute has been paid in the narrative; to those arbiters of our fortune, Major Bailey and Mr. Macdonald, I express once more our heartfelt thanks; but no man may set out on this journey untrammelled without being under an obligation to Mr. Percy Brown, whose wisdom and help in the preparation for the marches have lightened many a load, physical and mental, both for man and beast. The photographs illustrating this book are his work, and are an earnest of his knowledge of the frontier.

ILLUSTRATIONS

ILLUSTRATIONS

I

SILIGURI TO GANGTOK

When in the Club that evening I asked Dr. Bishop if he would come with me to Tibet, he merely assented and we proceeded with our conversation, for it is in that casual fashion that interesting events occur in one's life, and when some weeks later I reminded him of the conversation he told me that he had written to the Political Officer in Sikkim and that it was all right. In this way it happened that he and I, with two large boxes of food, two valises, two cameras and two pairs of glare-glasses, left Calcutta by the Darjeeling Mail early in the hot weather, on Good Friday evening, and settled down to *picquet* at a hundred roubles a point without much let or hindrance.

India has prepared many condiments for those who feed at her tables: fever, thirsts, greenfly and beggars: buffalo carts groaning along the dusty roads before an impatient motor car: legless *lalwallahs* that chew their *pan* at the level crossings, heedless of the frenzied hoots that bid them open: post office officials of all kinds: and above all, this matter of railroad travelling. She chooses the hottest and fiercest of days, and places an over-worked and over-irritated man in the dirtiest and shabbiest of carriages, and sends him hurtling through miles of dusty simmering country.

Dust, white, black and grey, clogs the creases in his hands, glues his collar to his neck, sticks his shoulders to his shirt, streams down his face, lies thick in his ears, and turns his snow-white trousers to the pepper and salt of a market farmer in his Sunday best. At the platforms sleeping men, in the wrappings of a corpse crying out for a much-needed burial, strew themselves before your path: *pan* chewers breathe their reek in your nose and spit their juice within an inch of your boots: cunning boxwallahs urge the purchase of their gewgaws from Benares: small naked boys beat upon their stomachs and cry out for rice money.

The train jangles on from station to station : the oven roars and blinds and roasts, and the everlasting panorama of earth, earth, earth, here a tree and there a cow, slips idly by.

At Paksey we came to the great suspension bridge and clanked noisily across. A faint breeze hung over the river, and I leant far out of the window and snuffed it up. I also uttered a prayer in honour of him that built the bridge, not because he had set up one of the longest and most graceful bridges of its kind, but in that he had persuaded the Ganges to flow under it after it was built.

Night came, and with it somewhat of a coolth and south breeze that filtered through the meat-safe window where dirt had not clogged. We changed over to the narrow gauge and continued our way in the luxury of a private saloon.

We stopped at a wayside station in the middle of the night, and voices broke in on our sleep: a high well-pitched voice, that meant others to hear besides its immediate listeners: 'Well, goodbye you fellows: thanks very much for seeing me off, don't you know. I hope you have a good time, and all that sort of thing.' Said I: 'That must be somebody going to Darjeeling for a month's leave—railway, I suppose.' Said Bishop: 'It sounds to me like one of the heaven-born of the new school saying goodbye to his babus,' and, alas, it was so.

At Paksey we collected the first member of the caravan, a Bengali sweeper whose chief qualification was the fact that he had no family ties; this recommendation had a certain grim humour which set us thinking. At Siliguri on the following morning we secured a cook-bearer, a good enough fellow, a Nepalese who had served with the Mount Everest Expedition and was rumoured to be a Christian.

We left Siliguri for Kalimpong Road by the Darjeeling-Himalaya Railway after an early breakfast. To appreciate the beauty of the scenery, the restfulness of trees and hedges, of stony paths and side-walks, one must spend some time beforehand in the plains of Bengal, and, for a full realisation of the great peace that one enjoys as the Teesta Valley slowly reveals itself, better preparation cannot be found than a sojourn of eighteen months in Calcutta.

The Teesta is not unlike a large salmon river in spate in Scotland. The water is greener, the shale is greyer, and there are trees; the boulders also are larger; but the hurry and scramble of the waters are the same, and spell the same secret—great fish lurking in deep pools.

So the train puffed its way up the twisting, wriggling track, now proclaiming its certainty that the next incline would be its last, now dashing forward with a shriek of excited triumph. We left it unhampered by our advice, and lolled back, our feet higher than our heads, computing how many pipes it would be necessary to smoke before we had sufficient nicotine to put on the tails of the leeches that would attach themselves to us during the march.

We reached the terminus at Kalimpong Road at noon, where we found our ponies and their syces, and a muleteer with two mules. The muleteer threw up his hands in consternation at the sight of our kit and loudly called for an extra mule, which he did not get, but had to content himself with a coolie whom he proclaimed as being sufficiently strong to carry a small basket to Rungpo.

Of the ponies, who were to be our most intimate companions, much might be written here, but it is better that their characters should be revealed slowly, just as they were revealed to us. Suffice for the present that Bishop's was a roan named Lucifer, and mine a black named Gyantse. Of the mules, one may say at once that fears suggested by previous army experience seemed groundless. They appeared to be orderly, peaceable creatures, standing placidly without admonishment or exhortation while our luggage and kit were piled upon them. One was grey, and highly respectable ; the other was black, and a *budmash.* The grey mule, in view of his great age and respectability, bore the heavier burden and intended to lead the caravan; the black mule, whose load was negligible, also intended to lead the caravan. And so, leaving the arbitration to the beasts themselves, we set out.

As we had no experience of the sort of thing mules and muleteers do, and as time was no object, we decided to keep with our baggage for that day at any rate, and pranced out uncomfortably in the mules' wake, where we witnessed that great struggle which is the epic of the Phari highway—the fight for the leadership. Epic of the countless shifts and devices concocted by the *budmash* mule so as to get one box at least in front of the grey mule; of the parrying and edging, and thrusting down slopes; of mad headlong career round corners; of jostling and stamping; of a slow sparring walk, eye to eye, and a sudden dash for supremacy: it occurs, is occurring at this moment, in every mule train that is moving along the way, whether it carries wool or kit, or some kazi collecting taxes, or an official from Lhasa prospecting in the Goutsa gorge for a site to build a mint. And the *budmash* mule, in the cool of the evening, left his respectable leader tired and jaded, and pirouetted to the front, and danced and ambled at will, feeding on dry and dusty leaves and bits of stick, heeding little the cautionary 'Tchu' and 'Tsa' jerked at him from the rear by the muleteer. But the grey mule plodded on, with the heavier load.

The road to Rungpo is good; a cart road following the right bank of the Teesta through woods and clearings. We rode at peace, spending most of the time in observing things that were to prove part and parcel of the day's work later. My pony at once revealed a trait in his character that could only be cured by the application of a bamboo switch, and, until that switch was cut and applied liberally, progress was considerably slower than it might have been. He also showed a peculiar aversion to ride by the side of Lucifer, and maintained that aversion to the end of the journey. This may have been due to the fact that before he was 'discovered' and trained for racing purposes he had been a pack pony in Gyantse and broken in for the mule train. He certainly had many traits of the mule in his nature, especially the virtue of being absolutely reliable in a stiff climb.

We were too early for flowers, but the road was as beautiful as one could wish, and in parts strangely reminiscent of the Ashdown Forest.

Towards evening our caravan was augmented by two kazis on their ponies and a group of coolie women with baskets. The muleteer, whether on account of the proximity of our destination or the bevy of ladies behind, burst into song, or snatches of yodel, greatly to our satisfaction and his own enjoyment, and gave tongue until sundown, when we reached the suspension bridge at Rungpo separating us from Sikkim. The bridge was closed for repair, but a makeshift had been rigged up. Here we fell in with a police patrol who collected our permits for Sikkim—and so we came to Rungpo.

Rungpo consists of a small collection of sheds and huts. Before one of these stood an exceedingly smart police corporal, who called himself to attention, saluted us with great zest and pointed the way to the dâk bungalow, some two hundred feet above the village.

This bungalow is certainly the best equipped, if not the most picturesque, to be met during the journey. It has a large verandah, excellent rooms, flowers, table-cloths, and baskets of orchids hanging from the eaves. Here we found tea and baths awaiting us and sat down in two long chairs, meditating on the day's march, and watching a blue mist slowly creep up and overshadow the gorge of the Teesta stretching before us. We discussed the question of that third mule, and felt that had we been anywhere else than at Rungpo that third mule would have been the burning topic of the hour.

There was a great peace in the valley, even though the mist meant to change to rain and spoil the next march.

TEESTA VALLEY

'Far below the waters of the Rongni Chu had decided to become a river.'

We turned in early, after further discussion as to the third mule. The night was hot and the mosquitoes devilishly keen on the fresh meat that the gods had sent them. I groped my way across my room and discovered a window, unnoticed before, but on opening it found to my disappointment that the mist had carried out its promise and rain was falling heavily.

It was still raining in the morning, but owing to delays due to the engagement of a coolie in place of the mule, and the despatch of a box of probable luxuries to Kalimpong in order to lighten our load, we did not get away until nine o'clock. The rain considerately stopped as soon as we were on the ponies, and we continued our march up the valley to Gangtok in comfort.

The Teesta valley here is cultivated, in small steps bordered with white stones. Far below we could distinguish five women in blue garments steadily marching in single file with great loads on their backs, reminding Bishop of the old story of the large ants that inhabited Tibet and grouted for gold, which he attributed to Herodotus.

Our first halt was Singtam, a village at the junction of the Rongni Chu with the Teesta. Singtam in some ways marks the end of familiar civilisation. One might say that the bridge that crosses the stream at the entrance of the village marks the entrance into the wilds, and that the long string of fluttering prayers, strips of cloth and ends of twisted paper, is really a defence to keep away stray bogies and outlanders.

The village is shaped like the letter T; it consists of native rest-houses, single-storeyed with thatched or wooden roofs. Each rest-house has a large verandah, on which merchants sit measuring the grain or weighing out other commodities: a carpenter making a table, a blacksmith hammering out flat a mule's shoe. Strangers are frequent here, and we attracted little attention. We sat and ate biscuits, while the muleteer and the syces explained to the villagers exactly what fit of madness had driven us into that part of the world.

After Singtam the valley becomes wilder; the stream winds through large white boulders, and the path passes underneath hanging cliffs. We left our mules and servants behind and rode on ahead. From this point onward, except on one occasion, that became the order of the day, and towards the end of a day's march we were at least two hours ahead of our servants. This has its disadvantages, for at times one must postpone the satisfaction of the inner man beyond the limits of one's temper, a fact that we were forced to feed upon more and more as we progressed on our journey.

Some three miles before Shamdong we started to climb. The road became less rugged and more earthy, and had a tendency to hang over the side of precipices, although our real introduction to the *khud* was not to come until much later. On the way up we passed the grave of a pioneer who had been accidentally killed in the construction of that road. He seemed a quaint link with the past, an early victim of the preparations that culminated in the Younghusband Expedition in 1904.

The Younghusband Expedition is still a very real tradition among all those who have been to Tibet or are connected with things Tibetan. But to me this solitary grave brought back a very different recollection of this tradition. It was in Lille Citadel in 1915, after the vigorous but somewhat abstruse operations that have been called the Battle of Loos.

A Gurkha officer, who had been captured on the first day of the battle, was standing in a doorway of the prison as I was brought in by my captors, and he received me with a doleful, sympathetic salaam.

From a strong sense of regimental duty I had read with care the history of the Younghusband Expedition, so that when I went down to walk some forty times round the courtyard on the following day and saw him smiling all over his face, and noticed the Tibetan ribbon on his coat, I went up to him and, knowing no Hindustani and he knowing no English, used the one magic word 'Younghusband.' His smile became a beam as he recognised my regimental badge, and in the incoherency of his answer I recognised the word 'Macdonald.' We became great friends, in spite of the limitation of our intercourse.

He had one philosophy of life, which was to draw a circle and put himself in the middle. In this way he explained to me the circumstances leading to his own capture at Loos: it also served to illustrate the discomfiture of the Tibetans at Tuna, Karo La and Gyantse. Later on he caused a serious breach of the peace by becoming a circle himself and putting some one else in the middle; it happened in this wise.

When orders came through for us to proceed to Germany, I, owing to an altercation with a German Staff Officer on the subject of a clothes-brush, was left behind at Lille as a hostage for the behaviour of some Indian prisoners; they had a barn full of Sikhs and Gurkhas and found them a trifle difficult. A few days later one of the Kaiser's artists came into the citadel with the express purpose of painting some of the oddities assembled there; and did me the honour to pass me by in favour of this Gurkha, as having greater possibilities. The Gurkha was quite pleased and, having removed his Balaclava helmet, stood in an extremely fierce posture before the artist, while I watched the progress of the portrait. It was an excellent piece of work; the man could certainly paint, and when he had finished I beckoned to the Gurkha to look at it. I have rarely seen a man's expression change to rage so instantaneously. He called up a companion, who at once shared his mortification. Owing to the action of the Balaclava and the natural fall of the hair the Gurkha's *ticki*, that single lock of hair, a parachute-ring in his flight to heaven, had become flattened, and had escaped the artist's notice; and so at one fell sweep of the brush a hopeful soul had been deprived of its means of transport. A brown streak drawn perpendicular to the crown placed matters once more on a friendly footing, but the artist had dallied enough with the British Army; he turned his attention to a French Colonial Officer.

On the whole I was not sorry to see the end of my Gurkha, for he and his party were more than a handful, especially in the train when we finally left for Germany. The Prussian subaltern in charge allowed them all to get out at a wayside station, with the result that they refused to get in again. He then meditated adding to the glamour of his second-class Iron Cross by falling upon them with the bayonet, so that it was high time to intervene. I took my Gurkha aside, drew a large circle and put him in the middle. A few minutes later we were steaming out of the station.

The men in those coaches were of the same stuff as those who, nearly twenty-five years ago, drew this great circle in the Himalayas and placed themselves in the middle, and the solitary Pioneer's grave seemed a more potent memorial of the work even than the road he had helped to build.

We pushed on to Shamdong, a rest-house built on the site of an old camp of the roadmakers, and found a polite kazi in a claret-coloured frock beaming at us from the road side. He seemed disappointed that we should ride through his village without going up to the bungalow for tiffin; but ride through we did, and halted a mile further up, at a cairn of stones built round a wooden post. We loosened our ponies' girths, tethered them to the post, and sat down to cocoa, biscuits and chocolate.

When we had finished our meal and had looked about us we were surprised to find that the cairn was really situated on the edge of a great precipice, and that the young bamboo growth had hedged it in and given it the appearance of a winding country lane; we were not able to discover whether the cairn had been erected as a memorial, or for some other purpose. Had the bamboos not been there we should have had an uninterrupted view of the whole of the Rongni Chu Valley from Singtam.

Some two miles below Shamdong the road divides, and there is a bridle-path, so called, leading to Gangtok, which saves three miles. Here we found our host for the coming night awaiting us with fresh ponies, Kunduling Cock and Aristocrat, stable-companions of Lucifer and Gyantse; and up that bridle-path we had our first experience of the Bhutia pony come into his own.

The thrill of the first moments of that scramble is indescribable, for walking and trotting in turns along the cart road from Kalimpong had not given us a hint of what these ponies are capable of doing. A scramble up paths built of boulders at impossible angles with impossible bends, hoofs clattering, bodies straining forward, all pressing for the leadership; a jostle and a scurry; the vigour of the moment seemed to grip every nerve in one's composition, and at every bound of the pony one felt endowed with a gift of new energy and new determination.

In the middle of the hot weather, when the Darjeeling season is at its height, the Bhutia ponies assemble from far and near for the races. Going is keen, and the form of the ponies well known, so that speculation is rife and much controversy rages in the bazaar as to the probable winners. Form is not the only standby, and many a good race has been upset by the favourites taking the order of proceedings into their own hands or mouths. Some bolt through the crowd and retire to their stables before the race is a minute old: others shed their jockeys on the race-course, leap the light wicker barricade and make for the bazaar at a gallop.

Both Kunduling Cock and Aristocrat had many wins to their credit and were favourites at the coming meeting, so that they were held back on this account from going with us into Tibet. On the road, or when trekking, Kunduling Cock would not tolerate any pony ahead of him, and Aristocrat accepted the situation and kept a length behind him: to do otherwise would have turned the simplest ride into turmoil: but on the race-course he was the faster pony, and went all out to win. Strangely enough the journey into Tibet had the effect of a tonic on Gyantse, for he carried all before him at the following meeting and beat his own more illustrious stable-companions, who had been kept behind to train for the occasion.

We arrived at Gangtok in time for an early tea, and spent the evening in discussing the road up which we were to travel, and the sort of thing to be expected of the road. Our host had been to Lhasa two years previously with Sir Charles Bell, and had recently returned from a shooting expedition in Bhutan, so that his knowledge of what was in store for us was considerable. Skins of leopard, snow-leopard and bear, all in the magnificent coat obtainable at such altitudes, showed what could be made of a journey into the Himalayas when one has time to linger on the way.

The mules arrived some three hours later, but the sweeper did not get in until half-past ten, having been regaled upon the way by stories of the heights he was to surmount and the great depth of snow he would be expected to cut his way through. He had already decided that 6,000 feet is quite high enough for the aspirations of any Bengali, however disreputable his caste or slender his family ties, and his low mind, fed by the cunning of the plains, was cogitating some plan whereby he might escape climbing the formidable barriers that stretched across his path: also he was very drunk.

II

GANGTOK

THE unbroken stretch of the Great Himalaya Range is the natural frontier of the Tibetans, and sufficiently forbidding for them to wish to respect its fastnesses. And yet, when the large finger groped forward from the Tibetan hand, and gently stroked Chumolaori into the hand's grasp, like some croupier at a gaming-table, it reached still further, and found the fertile valley of Chumbi, and settled in the valley. So that an oblong slice of territory some twenty miles broad and forty miles long, that should be Sikkim, is now Tibet. Geographically the Chumbi Valley is in Sikkim, and the bleak table-land of Phari should be the last outpost of Sikkim, that long dreary brown waste which stretches towards the Great Range and crosses into Tibet proper at the Tang La, 15,200 feet above sea-level.

The Chumbi valley is the highway for the Tibetans to Western civilisation by way of the marts of Kalimpong. At Chumbi or Yatung, which is also called Shashima, they meet the river Amo Chu and, turning half right, travel south-west over the passes Dzalep La or Nathu La to Sikkim and Kalimpong.

The history of the changes and chances that have led to the encroachments of the finger and the final dismembering of the Sikkim corpse is written on the stones of broken walls and bleak camps on the mountain-side. Here the Chinese had a wall, here the Tibetans pitched a camp, but as to the reason for the wall or the camp one need give little heed: inconsequent deeds are in keeping with the scenery that staged them, and it matters not if the Chinese or Tibetans held the keep.

Gangtok, at the head of the Rongni valley on the road to Tibet by the Nathu La, is the capital of the State of Sikkim and contains all that makes up a capital: the palace of the Maharajah, a monastery, a hospital and a jail. Far away to the south-west one can just distinguish Darjeeling; to the north-east is the range of hills, some 12,000 feet high, which threaten the path to the Donkhia Range and Tibet. They still have snow on them in early April, and, with the evening mist hanging over them or the black cloud that spells an early morning fall of snow, are grim enough. To the north-west, her great crest towering above intervening hills, lies Kinchenjunga, white and clear in the brilliant morning sun.

The first sight of snows and a real mountain is unforgettable. Often one has seen some great pile of tumbling white clouds and thought of it as a great mountain, but the real mountain has nothing of the cloud-dream about it. It is clear cut, sharp, grey, immensely old and immensely material, with a strange sense of cruelty that spells Mother Earth. Even when the foot of the range is covered in rolling snow-white cloud through which a few peaks thrust their heads, there is the same strange feeling of reality, of the triumph of the domain of men, of some hard material victory snatched from the world of spirit.

All these thoughts flashed through me as I surveyed Kinchenjunga from my dressing-room window; a brief triumph, for the clouds rose quickly and obscured her from view.

The hospital is a new memorial building, very modern and very clean, and though possessing no medical propensities I found myself looking with great interest at the odd collection of patients that had been sent from all corners of the State, and with still greater interest at the crude Japanese lithographs of the War which hung in the ward; ships were piled on ships and men on men; shells bursting and bayonets stabbing; in treatment akin to the medley of horses and men and clean lopped heads and arms that were the joy of the Mogul artists.

There was one little mite, with some disease or other that had been pronounced interesting, lying on her back contemplating the capture of Tsing Tau as visualised by a bazaar artist in Tokio. I wondered in how many combinations she had worked out the helmet spikes of the serried ranks of Germans, and how many times she had counted the perfect alignment of Japanese bayonets, and whether she had always made them tally.

Higher up the hill is a carpet factory, a large wooden shed where women were at work on blankets for the hospital. There were several carpets to be seen, one a large blue rug of simple design. On the whole they were disappointing, not on account of their texture or colours, but because the designs were tawdry. Plain carpets with little or no pattern are evidently considered unbecoming, and the results resemble the cheap wares offered by the manufacturers at home. This is a pity, for they have good colours to work from and a knowledge of the art of weaving. It is of course possible to have a carpet made to one's own design, but the design of a carpet is not the sort of thing one carries in one's head, and in any case design is a matter which should be left to the taste of the weaver. The attraction of a Persian rug lies not only in its superb workmanship; to submit a design to the weaver is as if one should take a love letter to a lyric poet and ask him to set it down in good verse.

As I was watching the women at work on the looms I stepped back suddenly and struck my foot against something very hard. A faint whimper followed and looking down I found I had kicked the head of a baby lying asleep on the floor. Its mother seemed unperturbed and the baby decided not to squall, but when I returned that way later I noticed that it was hastily gathered up and deposited out of my reach. To our great joy five dirty children made faces through the door while the woman in charge proudly showed her treasures. Mindful of our wretched sweeper we entered into negotiations for a cardigan jacket, and while this was in progress the Secretary to the Maharajah came to see us.

He was a large, impressive person, rather grim of feature, but with a curious glint in his eyes which suggested a sense of humour differing from Western standards. Obviously shrewd and cool-headed, and obviously determined; an able man who was prepared to take from his Western neighbours just as much of their habits and philosophy as suited his convenience, and no more. He had a very charming manner, and spoke English perfectly. He was dressed in a blue silk Chinese robe with long sleeves, and a blue silk underskirt, and wore his hair in a long plait. In his company we climbed the hill to the Maharajah's palace.

The palace is a large square building of two storeys, gaily decorated in Chinese fashion and painted in bright colours, blue, red, yellow and green. The ground floor is taken up for the most part by a large temple, containing an image of the *guru*, the instructor of the Buddha. Before the *guru*, as an aid to his contemplation, were the seven bowls of brown porcelain with Chinese characters embossed in gold, containing holy water, and near by sat a lama, the guardian and attendant of the temple, offering prayers and reading from the holy books. There is a quietness and peace in Buddhist temples, an atmosphere of age-old philosophy and calm meditation. There is also an atmosphere of grimness helped very much by the architecture. A low dark building with great wooden beams supporting the roof: two low beams to act as seats for the lamas, who sit in a row up the centre of the temple each side of the Buddha. A collection of books—manuscripts folded between strips of wood and inserted each in its own pigeon-hole—a banner or two, a large unwieldy foghorn to keep away demons, and the indispensable tea-pot: these formed the furniture of the temple. On the lawn in front were stretched the gaudy blue robes for the devil dancers, drying in the sun in readiness for the approaching festival, and some men and women were engaged in erecting a stage. A wandering Tibetan beggar, with cymbals and grotesque mask, was dancing before the palace. He kept up a quaint, mournful dirge and executed certain interminable treadmill gyrations.

The Maharajah himself lives in the Summer Palace, a modern

house furnished in European style some fifty yards from the Winter Palace, as the large house on the hill is called. We found him sitting in a small drawing-room, waiting for us. He has an intellectual face, has read a great deal and interests himself chiefly in his religion and the people. He is a friend and admirer of the Trashe Lama, the spiritual head of the Tibetan Buddhists, who directs lama thought from Shigatse and is as much venerated by the Tibetans as the Dalai Lama himself. In 1904, when the Dalai Lama escaped from Lhasa in face of the Younghusband expedition, the Trashe Lama took over the control of Lamaism, and the same Chinese proclamation that deposed the Dalai Lama vested the spiritual power in the Trashe Lama. This spiritual power he retained after the expulsion of the Chinese in 1912.

The Maharajah had received that morning a letter with two photographs from the Trashe Lama at Shigatse; the sight of the Kodak Printing Paper envelope which contained them and the fact that it had come from such a man and from such a place seemed most incongruous.

It is this devotion to his religion that has made the present Maharajah so popular with his people. He succeeded to the throne after the early death of his brother, who, having acquired at Oxford ideas out of keeping with the simple philosophies of Gangtok, had the misfortune —as the Secretary expressed it—to die soon after his return to his State. His successor, with the exception of visits to Calcutta and Delhi, has not travelled extensively, nor, bearing in mind his brother's experience, does he wish to do so. In any case, apart from the question of expense, for the Sikkim exchequer is a poor one, it is difficult for a man of the

Maharajah's religious convictions to travel anywhere with any degree of comfort, for the ways of omens and soothsayers are strange, and have little in common with the requirements of modern civilisation. Thus when one's southward way is blocked by spirits and bogies of evil intention it may be necessary to travel due north for a space of ten miles in order to deceive them, to climb some distant hill or ford some obscure river; if two are travelling together the chance of deception will be enhanced if they leave their house by different doors and their garden by different gates: if they meet at a point some six miles out of their course so much the better: if the baby is to accompany them, let him not go out of the door at all, and that will complete the by-play—so the baby goes out by the window and joins his parents on a third diverging path, and one can hoot at the bogies for a parcel of fools. Unfortunately we saw neither the wife nor the baby, for the former was doing her hair, a long and formidable operation.

On the northern crest of the hill of Gangtok, overlooking the valley and the great sweep of the hill and mountain, is the monastery of Enchë, a square red-roofed wooden building. Before it wave a hundred prayers, fluttering in the breeze from tall bamboos. '*Om mane padme hum*' ('Hail to the jewel, and the lotus'). A lama in a thick dirty brown cassock, with curling hair and beard and an eye gleaming with fun, was in attendance, accompanied by a small boy novice, a kind of 'chela.' He showed us the quiet bare temple, where Buddha sat calmly and placidly. A faint glimmer of light from small votive lamps, woollen wicks, floating in bowls of oil, lit up the gloom of one corner of the temple. Before the Buddha were six bowls only of holy water, for a thief had taken the seventh; and that the lack of it should not interrupt the meditations of the Buddha they had hung from a beam a large coloured ball, a cheap Christmas decoration bought for an anna in the Kalimpong bazaar, on which he might gaze in calm oblivion. The lama considered that the gaudy coloured ball, in strong contrast to the beautifully chased bowls of porcelain, provided a more effective stimulus to the image's devotions.

There seemed to be a great peace in the six bowls of unruffled water, the transparent quiet of the ball, the dark silent temple, the steady glow of the oil lamps, and the grim forbidding look of the wooden beams and unswept ceiling.

Outside the wind whistled, the rain poured down, the heavy sodden prayer flags flapped from their poles. Man is so much in contact with the elements in Sikkim and Tibet; his life is one great conflict against mountains that brook no crossing: earth that gives no food: snow, ice, hail and burning sun; it is little wonder that he has turned animist: that implacable demons and fiends seem ever to be seeking for his destruction, haunting the wild mountain side, raging among the mountain torrents, mocking him from the snows and smiting crops with hailstones as soon as he has coaxed the crops from the unwilling soil. It is a land of stone and rock, and so that dreary wail of praise—'Hail to the jewel and the lotus'—is sent up everlastingly, in wheels at the porches of the temples, in wheels by the hands of devoted lamas, in wheels by the hands of traveller, beggar and herdsman; by a hundred flags on cairn and crest, by a thousand fluttering strips of cloth across river and torrent, strips of cloth caught up in bushes or nailed to trees.

Om mane padme hum (Hail to the jewel and the lotus)—a strange cry for pity, for consolation to those who can strive against and conquer the demons, a pathetic cry, a wistful cry wrung from those who have no vision of the jewel or of the lotus, only of relentless cold, hail, wind, rain, snow, barrenness—a great conspiracy of bogies hatched in this glorious expanse of beauty. *Om mane padme hum*—but they gaze into the face of the Medusa.

So when your crops are eaten up by the hail, you climb the hill to the monastery and give gifts of kind and money to the good lamas, and the large fog-horn is produced from the recesses of the temple, and a hideous din is made with it, hurled across valleys, echoing through the mountains: and, if the hail stops, your climb and money have had a good return: and if the hail continues, then surely your enemies have given more money, richer gifts to another monastery, and the demons are driven your way by a bolder clatter: and so you climb the hill once more, with more money and richer gifts, and the horn re-echoes down the valley once more and up through the hills, and one day the hail will stop: *Om mane padme hum.*

A picturesque place is Gangtok, perched on its hill at the head of the Rongni valley, and the jewel in its crown is the Residency, with its roses, orchids and dovecot: polished oak floors, pictures, books: great fireplaces, an English country house hidden away in the hills of India.

The Sikkimese are a happy lot, in spite of the bogies and the elements. Marriage is a thing that does not bother them much. A woman may have a couple of husbands if she likes or more, and nobody

CHUMBI VALLEY

'Life is one great conflict against mountains that brook no crossing, earth that gives no food.'

quarrels about it. Polyandry here and in Tibet is a cheerful kind of business, and the women pay for the privilege by doing most of the work. They are a healthy lot, tall, muscular and smiling: hoydens: much of the type of the seventeenth century Dutch peasant woman that Jan Steen loved to paint: a laughing young hussy in Chumbi, lugging one husband along by the arm while two tried to pull him the other way, and a fourth sought to put his arm round her waist: it was a jolly sight, very much the sort of thing that would have appealed to Ostade or Jan Steen, and the costumes were as much in keeping with the picture as the big-boned, deep-bosomed young woman who inspired it.

The revenue of the State is poor, for wealth is in the hands of the kazis, and it is difficult to get them to disburse it, or to assess the amount they are liable to disburse. A tax on *bustis*—the low mud huts of India—would be simple, if an accurate return of *bustis* could be given. Stern measures have been resorted to in order to secure an accurate return. The tax was fixed at five rupees for each *busti* and the kazis were requested to hand in their contributions. On settling day, when the returns had been rendered, the kazis were informed that a census would be taken and the returns checked with the official figures. A fine of one hundred rupees would be levied for the first *busti* not registered, and a further fine of fifty rupees for each subsequent unregistered *busti*. One kazi excused himself from the gathering on hearing of that census, went off to count again, and discovered to his surprise that he had two hundred more *bustis* in his possession than he had expected.

We stayed for one day only at Gangtok, and left it on the following morning for the march proper to Phari Dzong. Our host had made a careful *bundabast* for the mules. Four altogether were necessary, with a muleteer in charge: two for our baggage, one for fodder, and one for servants' baggage and general *impedimenta.* They were to accompany us to Phari Dzong and return with us to Kalimpong Road Station. A sum inclusive of all expenses—mules, muleteer, fodder, food and stabling—was fixed with the kazi: a deposit was paid: and we congratulated ourselves on having made such a *bundabast* as would relieve us from all transport worries during the expedition—these were our salad days, when hope beat high!

A jingle of bells during the latter stages of breakfast advised us that the mules had arrived. There were six of them, for that is the custom of the country, to bring more than the number stipulated and to allow the contracting parties, after endless argument, to settle between them which seem the least unfit. A long rope with a stake at each end was stretched on the ground: the stakes were driven in and each mule was hobbled to the rope by the right fore-leg. The mule at the end of the row was as miserable a specimen as one could hope to see: small, thin, knock-kneed, heavily ribbed: a jaded eye and a mouth made for yawning. I at once demanded that he should be thrown out. The muleteer was flabbergasted: '*Bahut accha wallah hai, Sahib*' ('A very fine fellow, Sir'), and he burst into a torrent of Sikkimese. When translated his arguments were certainly potent. He said that that mule ate less corn, less grass and did more work than any other mule in Sikkim: and he backed his opinion by giving it the heaviest load. He was certainly justified. If ever beast aspired rightly to that term of 'accha wallah' it was that mule. It carried the heaviest load daily without complaint: it always looked on the point of death: it always nearly died a mile before our destination: it just did not expire on reaching its stable. It walked slowly and painfully in the rear of the caravan: it turned neither to the right nor the left: it showed no sign of life nor interest in life: it made no complaint and lifted not its voice: and it ate less corn than one can cram into a decent-sized cigarette tin.

The leader was an old hand, a brown mule with one large bell: the second mule had a great string of bells, and provided the music on the way: the third mule was insignificant and had no bell: nor had the miserable specimen: perhaps he would have tolled his own knell on it.

All was in readiness except the servants' baggage, and the leading mule was still without a load: since it was to bear the responsibilities of the journey it was kept as light as possible. The servants' bundles lay on the ground, an easy load for this sage and active beast, once they had been tied into a compact bale. The muleteer tried to tie them, but the thong—a long strip of tough bark—snapped as soon as it was drawn round. This obstacle overcome, the muleteer tried to lift the bundle, but failed: then the *mali*, attracted from his orchids by the violence of the discussion, tried to lift it and failed—and they both decided that it contained iron. This intrigued the mules immensely, especially the miserable specimen, who looked at it lovingly, wondering why it could not be substituted for or added to the ton or so already piled on its back. At last the muleteer and the *mali* and the two syces put their shoulders to the bundle, hoisted it and deposited it on the leader's back. We were ready to start.

So we set out once more, ourselves with our host leading, the mules jingling behind us to whoops and cries from the muleteer and the syces; in the rear, Tchugro, the cook, with a smile on his face indicating his contempt for our turn-out when compared with the pretensions of his former expedition, and the sweeper, very self-conscious in his new puttees, both carrying umbrellas. We wound up the hill until we could look down on the whole of Gangtok, on the two wooded crests, on Enchë and the Palace and the stream sparkling far down in the valley. Here we said goodbye to our host and followed the path towards the Nathu La and the table-land of Tibet.

III

KARPONANG AND CHANGU

From Gangtok to Karponang is a short march of about ten miles, so we started quite late. We parted from our host at the fifth mile-post and at once began to climb. The valley was broad, open and stony, and the road climbed steadily for two miles.

At the seventh milestone we had our first experience of a verandah bridge. The road, cut in the side of the mountain, stops abruptly in front of a sheer precipice, too sheer for a path to be cut. Stakes are driven into the mountain and across these stakes long planks are laid; the interstices are filled up with mud and small stones, and a hand-rail completes the deception of a bridge. A most ricketty contraption, to be tackled with considerable trepidation at first, before nerves are settled and familiarity has bred contempt.

It is wise to lead one's pony over these verandah bridges, not so much because the possible lack of nerves above mentioned may cause one to take a header over the hand-rail, but because the mud and small stones that fill up the gaps between the planks get washed away; a pony's foot may slip through the bottom of the bridge, and the header becomes a certainty.

So we walked our ponies over this verandah bridge, which swayed ominously, and regained the road on the opposite side, where, feeling rather proud of ourselves, we sat down to boiled eggs and cocoa.

The road from Gangtok to Karponang is not the most beautiful stretch in the march, but it is interesting, for in it one is subjected for the first time to all those experiences which are to become part of the day's routine later, although not met with in the even tenor of the average way. Of these the most alarming is the *Khud*, the precipice overhung by a path cut out of the side of the mountain.

This overhanging path varies in breadth from ten feet, which is a comfortable breadth, to eighteen inches, which is cutting it rather fine. In civilised parts of the world, such as parts of Sikkim, especially the road to Tibet over the Dzalep La on the Sikkim side, it has been made up with large flat stones, well laid and levelled at a slant towards the side mountain, like the bend on a *luge* run. The breadth of this made-up *khud*, for *khud* implies the combination of path and precipice, is rarely less than six feet, and a very safe and comfortable path would be the result were it not for the perversity of the Bhutia pony.

The Bhutia ponies are generally 'discovered' as pack animals or riding ponies in the mule trains bringing wool from Tibet. They are taught to emulate the habits of a mule, and any propensity for deviating from the habits of a mule that they may show, such as cantering or trotting, is carefully thrashed out of them. The reason for this is that the Tibetan saddle is really a perch, a pile of bedding on which the kazi balances himself, his knees drawn up halfway to his chin. A canter would dislodge him at once, a trot would place him in an extremely awkward predicament, and reduce his working parts to the consistency of a beaten egg; so the pony is trained to walk and to amble only, and a high price is paid for a good ambler. If one rides in the orthodox English fashion this same amble develops into a form of torture.

The Bhutia pony is trained for the mule train, and he conducts himself as a mule. He walks at a steady even pace, and ambles when occasion demands: he also possesses one other of the mule's idiosyncrasies. For the mule is a beast with curiosity, and he finds a strange fascination in gazing over space, in hanging over the precipice the utmost ounce of his body consistent with the law of equilibrium: so he revels in the *khud*. He walks on the extreme edge of the *khud*, with half his body, half his pack, his head and, if possible, at least two feet hanging over the side. If the road is rough, loose, obviously dangerous, he will linger lovingly on it: push his head over the side and drink in the scene in the valley two thousand feet below. If the road is good, built up, but has below its edge soft loose earth, which has not yet crumbled or been washed away in the valley, he will leave the road and walk on that loose earth. And the Bhutia pony who has started life in a mule train, even if in the meantime he has been trained to polo and racing and has all the tricks of galloping, cantering and trotting at his elbow, will revert to the habits of the mule when he gets to the *khud* again, and walk on the edge and amble and play his tricks.

At first these tricks are alarming: to feel half of one's body hanging over the edge: there is a strong tendency to keep one's neck rigid and stare straight to one's front, although one knows that the beast is sure-footed, and perfectly happy: going his own way in his own land.

All these things are first experienced on the way to Karponang, and the preliminary terrors overcome during that stretch of road which lies between the eighth and ninth milestones. Here the *khud* is very typical: the mountain side bare and stony, the valley some thousand feet below, the path strewn with boulders and loose earth.

I was riding some two hundred yards behind my companion. The road was steep, and I had long given up any attempt to keep Gyantse in the middle of the path. We had been climbing for the last hour at an even walk. The steady movements of the pony, the rhythmic clatter of his hoofs and the quiet calm of our surroundings had produced a kind of lethargy in me; my thoughts were very far away. Suddenly there was a rustle in front of us, a boulder with loose earth crashed on to the path a few yards ahead, Gyantse was on his knees and I was rolling over on the path: fortunately I had come off on the side opposite the *khud*, otherwise these words would not have been written.

It took me some time to recall my wits, and I felt very shaken when I picked myself up; I sat down on a boulder for a minute or two, waiting for my breath to come again, for the suddenness of my fall had left me sick and dizzy. Gyantse was unhurt, but frightened.

Landslides seem to be the one thing that these ponies are really afraid of, and the toll claimed in horses, mules and men in a year on this account must be heavy. I led the unwilling Gyantse past the cause of our accident, mounted again and was glad to get clear of that stretch of road. I learnt from that incident to gather my wool in more suitable places.

The slight drizzle which habitually comes on in the early afternoon, when the clouds that have gathered in the valleys have had time to climb to the tops of the hills, now started. In a driving mist we pushed on to the rest-house, a wooden building perched on the hillside amid a cluster of wooden outhouses, and reached it at three o'clock.

We soon got a large log-fire going, stabled our ponies and waited for the mules. As we waited we looked over the Visitor's Book and were much amused to read the complaint of a certain Russian Princess, who had made the tour of the Passes in 1921 with a companion. She complained of draughts, a lack of curtains and general niceties of civilisation. These complaints were far from our own thoughts, which tended to the singing of paeans to him who strewed dak bungalows in the path of travellers, or to primitive man, who discovered the comfort afforded by great logs burning in a great hearth. Curiously enough these ladies had already crossed Bishop's path in Mesopotamia and Persia, where they had travelled considerably during the latter months of the War. The foreign lands bordering the remote confines of the British Empire seem to have an irresistible attraction for them.

The mules arrived about an hour later, and the jingle of their bells aroused us from our lethargy. We went to the door and found that the clouds had lifted still further, and everything was clear.

The Karponang bungalow lies at the head of the gorge of the Rongni Chu. It is a little below the snow line. The pine-clad hills and great overhanging boulders were a feast of colours: greens, blues and dark purples. Overhead a turquoise sky: to the north the great mass of cloud rolling upwards towards the summit of the Himalayas.

Opposite on the other side of the gorge a great buttress of mountain bulged southwards, and round this buttress wound the road that we were to take on the morrow: a narrow path dividing into two, one upper and one lower, marking the snow line round the hill. We could trace it from where we stood, chiselled out of the side of the hill, now shaded by trees, now bleak with snow, now crossing some frozen waterfall, now clinging to the bare mountain side, now a verandah bridge overhanging the valley. We could trace it for some three miles as it crept round the buttress, as far as the Lagyap La where, the buttress rounded, it turns north-east again and climbs to Lake Tanye Tso, to Changu and Nathu La.

The prospect of that path was as beautiful as one can hope to see. Above it was the snow-clad crest of the buttress: far below the waters of the Rongni Chu had decided to become a river, had gained shape and direction, and were gliding like some huge serpent towards the great Rangit River, towards Teesta, towards Ganges, towards the sea.

The evening drew on and we turned into the bungalow. On the verandah an abject sight awaited us. There sat the sweeper in complete kit, plus two blankets: his puggaree entwined over his Balaclava: mournfully contemplating the snow-clad line of mountains, to cross which was to be his bitter lot on the morrow. He complained that he had forgotten his boots, and could go no further. But the *Chowkidar*, for the sum of annas eight, produced two uppers that owned no soles and two soles that owned no uppers, and Bishop produced his medicine chest. The sweeper blanched at the sight of the bottles and instruments; and when two bandages were produced he made ready to give

KARPONANG

' The pine-clad hills were a feast of colours : greens, blues, and dark purples.'

up his life. The uppers were drawn over his feet, the soles clapped on. While I held them fast Bishop wound his bandages across and around, and so our sweeper was well and truly shod, like a cat in paper shoes. Tchugro came out to inspect him. 'Do you see that?' he asked, jerking his thumb towards a snow-clad peak some seventeen thousand feet high. 'We are going over it to-morrow.' Then he bade him good-night with a smile.

On the morrow we left the rest-house at nine o'clock, a glorious morning, cloudless, brilliant with colour. We decided to take the upper road and had started to climb by a zigzagged causeway when the shouts of the syces and the yodelling of the muleteer from below warned us that the path had given way further on and was impassable. We came down with some reluctance and resumed the lower path. Later on the remains of a large landslide marked the place where a stretch of the upper path had collapsed and tumbled into the valley, carrying trees and boulders in its course and damaging the lower path.

Snow lay here and there, for we were on the edge of the snow line, and the road consisted chiefly of verandah bridges and loose earth. There were sudden bends and turns, with overhanging boulders, and Gyantse turned these blind corners with a great show of reluctance, as if fearing the bogies that lurked behind them.

At one point we turned and found the path descending steeply by a series of verandah bridges to a bamboo bridge across a great waterfall, and mounting again to the snow level beyond.

Here, winding down from the opposite side of the valley, a long train of mules loaded with wool slowly plodded towards the bridge.

Their bells jingled and filled the whole valley, before so silent, with a faint murmur, and the mules as they scrambled down the path to the bridge, appeared and disappeared like flashes of light in the gaps among the trees.

They were led by two stalwart Tibetan peasants, with hideous, swollen faces; their eyes covered by giant spectacles, their great tongues lolling out in the amenities of an early morning salaam. The mules clashed and stuck with our own at the bridge, and there was much rushing and shooing before our mules were packed side by side in a neat line with their noses over the *khud*. The train went by individually with mad rushes and scampers, jostling our mules with their packs of wool, driven forward in a frenzy by the yells of the muleteers. It was a confused and disturbed scene, and I marvelled why half of them did not go over into the valley. In their rear rode the kazi, an old and gnarled Tibetan on a shaggy pony. Both master and beast were dressed in gay trappings, and looked extremely business-like, especially the former, in spite of the benevolent aspect imparted to him by his long white hair. For he carried a long-barrelled flint-lock, a weapon spelling danger to its possessor, and met our greetings with a ferocious glare.

The road up from the bridge was bad and continued to be bad until we came to the place where it rejoins the upper road. This marked the end of the buttress which had been visible from Karponang, and we turned into the Changu valley after a last look at the Rongni Chu.

Vegetation had now ceased; a few blasted pines and withered

rhododendron twigs, that could have known no leaves and precious little sap, were all the signs of life visible. The road was good and the valley continued straight and open as far as the sixteenth mile from Gangtok, where it branches into two. At this point are the remains of a camp of the 1904 expedition, a small plateau of about an acre of withered grass, close cropped, and brown mud; well sheltered from the north by a bend in the valley.

A *ghuddi* or tea-house stands at the junction of the roads, and the road itself merges into the valley. For the Rongni Chu here is a trickle of water, and the valley into which we had turned had been climbing steadily until it had reached the level of the road. Henceforth the valley and the road were one, and the sides of the valley, covered with snow and blasted tree-stumps, were only one thousand feet high, of which about three hundred were visible. The breadth of the valley from hill to hill could not have been more than four hundred yards, and very straight and desolate it seemed.

From the edge of the camp, where we sat and munched chocolate, we could look back down the valley along the sides of which our road had wound; on the trickle of water that tumbled down to help swell the serpent that we had seen from Karponang. A blue mist was rising in the far distance, the herald of the afternoon cloud, and emerging from the mist we could see an insignificant cone-shaped hill with a square white speck on it: this was Gangtok.

The valley was warm though desolate. Under the large boulders were clusters of primulas and a small yellow flower resembling a dandelion. Snow became more frequent, and took the form of drifts rather than patches; soon it became a carpet, obscuring even the primulas; rock took the place of earth, and barren waste had caused even the blasted pine-trunks to disappear.

The road was cut out of the rock; it was slippery and treacherous. The valley climbed higher and higher, and the side of the ravine seemed more undulating. We were coming to the crest of the barrier, to the summit of that line of mountains, 13,000 feet high, which had looked so formidable from Gangtok.

The mist had now rolled up and reached us; before us the ravine ended abruptly in a great dam of rock over which streams of water trickled gently. The air was damp and cold, the mist became cloud, and there was a feeling of cheerlessness and desolation.

We climbed over the dam and found, stretching for half a mile before us, the frozen Lake of Tanye Tso. The path ran by the edge of the lake, the ice was thin with a covering of snow: there were gaps here and there through which black water gleamed. A grey boulder at the lake-side marked the twentieth milestone from Gangtok; it was a place to sadden a Satyr.

The mist changed to cloud, the cloud changed to drizzling rain, and the rain changed to hail. It seemed to be the end of the world, a jumping-off place to some fresh experience: a creepy waste where nothing that had happened in life seemed to matter. The dark gloomy lake and the barren mountains of earth and boulder that enclosed the lake formed a large bowl, a basin perched on the top of the earth, in which a man might be held while the ghost within him was forcibly and painfully extracted and driven to roam round the basin until it

BELOW CHANGU

'Sudden bends and turns, with overhanging boulders.'

had found the edge and whatever was beyond; a place for a frightened ghost to linger and tremble.

We pushed on for the rest-house, which lay at the head of the lake. A dismal wooden hut, two-roomed, it offered shelter from the hail and hopes of a fire, which were nobly fulfilled, although the smoke declined to go up the chimney and preferred to wander about the bungalow and through the chinks and gaps in the walls until it linked with the mist outside. It was barely one o'clock and yet the cloud gloom gave an impression of evening. There was no hope of the mules for an hour, so we sat waiting for the cloud to lift, and played picquet for the increased stakes of 1.000 rouble points. Upon the arrival of the mules we ate a large tiffin and sat and read. By four o'clock we discovered that the clouds had climbed above us, and found the lake clear and visible, but not kindly, for it looked bleak in spite of the colours of the rocks in the mountain sides flanking the Changu Valley.

Both of us complained of headaches and turned in early with the determination of getting away on the next morning at a quarter to seven, so that we could reach the top of the Pass at eight o'clock, before any cloud had collected in the distant valleys. We hoped for an uninterrupted view of Chumolaori and Kinchenjunga and, with many exhortations, turned in at an early hour, glad of any article of raiment to pile on our beds, and pulling our woollen helmets over our ears, for the cold was extreme.

IV

THE NATHU LA

THE next morning, owing to unavoidable delay, we did not succeed in getting away until eight o'clock, well wrapped up, with spares in the shape of woollen helmets and mufflers in our haversacks. There had been a heavy fall of snow during the night and the ponies had difficulty in keeping to the track, which was barely eighteen inches broad. In the end Lucifer refused to march in it, and plunged about in the drifts on each side of the track, which were from three to four feet deep. The only thing that could be done was to send the mules ahead to clear a path and march behind them. This ruse succeeded, for they trampled out a narrow track of some fifteen inches through the snow along which the ponies, save for occasional excursions into likely-looking drifts, were content to follow.

The road was broken and narrow, and our attentions were confined to the difficulties it offered; it led from mountain top to mountain top, over crests and round buttresses of stone. The mountain crests were too close to one another for a long sweeping view: and they looked decidedly grim and barren. At length after a long detour round the crest of a hill, we found a ravine stretching before us at the head of which lay Nathu La.

The approach to the Nathu La and the Pass itself are not formidable: the last stages of road are veritable road and not an iniquity, as is the approach to the Dzalep. The approach has been so gradual that there is no need for a formidable climb, and save for the actual scramble over the snow-covered pass, the way is easy enough.

The Pass, when compared with the Dzalep La, is rarely used and is not open all the year. The road itself is a natural path made by countless feet of mules; when we crossed, it had been opened only a week. The snow was from three to four feet deep, and frozen. Over this frozen and slippery path lay a foot of fresh snow, representing the fall of the previous night. This fall, which in the early stages of the march had completely obliterated the path, at this stage merely made it treacherous. For the path had been hacked or trampled down through large drifts, so that a bank of snow lay each side and the footholds and strong places where man or mule might tread in safety were obliterated; there was much stumbling and holding up and whistling and hallooing by all concerned.

The Pass itself seemed to be retreating before us. Time after time we surmounted what we had hoped to be the final crest, only to find another crest confronting us with the obvious appearance of being our coveted goal. At one point we were nearly all swept down in a tumbling mass of beasts, men and odd limbs into the valley beneath—it happened in this wise.

The mules had tired, and were scrambling up with great reluctance, so much so that the leading mule wished to argue the advisability of advancing further, and always chose an awkward moment for his protests. At one point in the way we came to a most hazardous turn, where the road was nearly perpendicular and afforded no foothold for the ponies, and little attraction for the mules. They seemed to slip back two feet for every foot they climbed, so that our position was precarious: we could only grip hard, keep quiet, and not be too anxious about the 500 feet or so of sheer drop beneath. It was a moment for a brisk and thoughtless scramble, but the leading mule cleared the steep and stood still! Nothing would move him. He refused to budge until he had regained his breath and enjoyed the picturesque nature of his surroundings. And we were left clinging to the ice at an angle of eighty degrees, like drunken flies with elastic legs; hoofs slithering and slipping; ponies showing a tendency to lose their heads; the three mules in front inclined to faint and fall back load and all upon the top of us. It was a moment of varying emotions. The muleteer had experience of such moments, and started to fling snowballs right and left. He seemed to be glued to the mountain side, to be breaking shop-windows from the cover of the village pillar-box, and he got the mule on the back of the neck with such effect that the beast actually moved. A scramble and a bound forward by all of us: for a moment we thought we were clear. But the miserable specimen of mule, who had regarded the last proceedings as a favourable opportunity for giving up the ghost thrown away, was not to be outdone by his leader; he stopped in his turn to recover, not his breath but his life, and no snowball could shift that gallant frame. We were left in a worse predicament, for the snow had been turned into glass by the slipping and backsliding of those who had been held up in front of us previously. It seemed as if nothing could save us from being carried away. Then the ponies made a sudden leap upwards and carried mule and all forward to safety; but we were well pleased to clear that hazardous turn.

Once we were clear, I dismounted and stumbled forward gaily over what I took to be the Pass. But another range awaited us beyond, and it was fifteen minutes before we stood by the cairn of stones that marked the Nathu La.

Round the cairn stood a few strips of bamboo with prayer flags tied to them, and a yak's tail fluttered from the cairn itself, although it was not the yak's tail that engaged our attention.

Behind us was nothing but mist; clouds had obscured the gorge up which we had climbed. Before us, as far as the eye could see, stretched Tibet, cloudless, gleaming in the midday sun. Range upon range, furrow upon furrow, stretched the brown barren hills, picked out in chocolate and black, clear-cut and distinct each from each, the sun gilding the crests and throwing them forward in relief from their fellows behind, like furrows in a giant's field, or neat and orderly plaster hills on a relief map. Behind them, thrusting a mighty spire ten thousand feet into the cloudless sky, snow-clad, ineffable, Chumolaori, divine mother of mountains. One pure white spire towering above those furrows of chocolate and black, rich chocolate, rich black, and the whiteness of snow. Above all a cloudless sky, not blue but turquoise, a vista of mighty jewellery, glittering beneath an Eastern sun.

The wind swept cold and pure, cut against our faces, whistled in our ears, filled our eyes with tears, but all unheeded as we gazed at the marvel stretched before us. For all doubts faded, and all fears were dispelled; before us stretched immortality, purification, a revelation of the world as God sees it, where no man has stepped to mar it—*Om mane padme hum* !

No wonder that men creep in paltry numbers on the face of it, or hide in holes beneath the surface of it. Here is a place where man is of no avail; where a close analysis and investigation of his soul is a task to draw tears of pity. Man dwells upon the face of it, an intruder; above it stretches the divine mother of mountains, unconquered, untrampled, untrammelled—Chumolaori: the purest gem in that mighty diadem.

At one's side, the paltry cairn thrown up by a passing peasant, the yak's tail, the bamboo canes, the fluttering prayers: a gale of wind would sweep them headlong. But the winds pent up in the plains of that table-land of Tibet, caught in her hollows, compressed in her mountain cups, rage and shriek to no purpose around Chumolaori. She stands there serene, immovable, unconquerable: a prayer of God, that can only be gazed upon in wonder: simple as that other prayer of God: a snow-white peak, solitary, magnificent, towering ten thousand feet above the place where man can tread.

We started the descent into Tibet in silence: leaping from crag to crag, splashing through the thaw that was snow, following a trickle of water that served as a road. A mule left the track and wallowed in a deep drift; the syces ran to the rescue, but we passed on unheeding : if the devils of that land demanded a mule as a sacrifice, they should have it. The beast was dragged out kicking from some five feet of snow. The great chocolate ridges welled up to the sky as we scrambled down

CHUMOLAORI

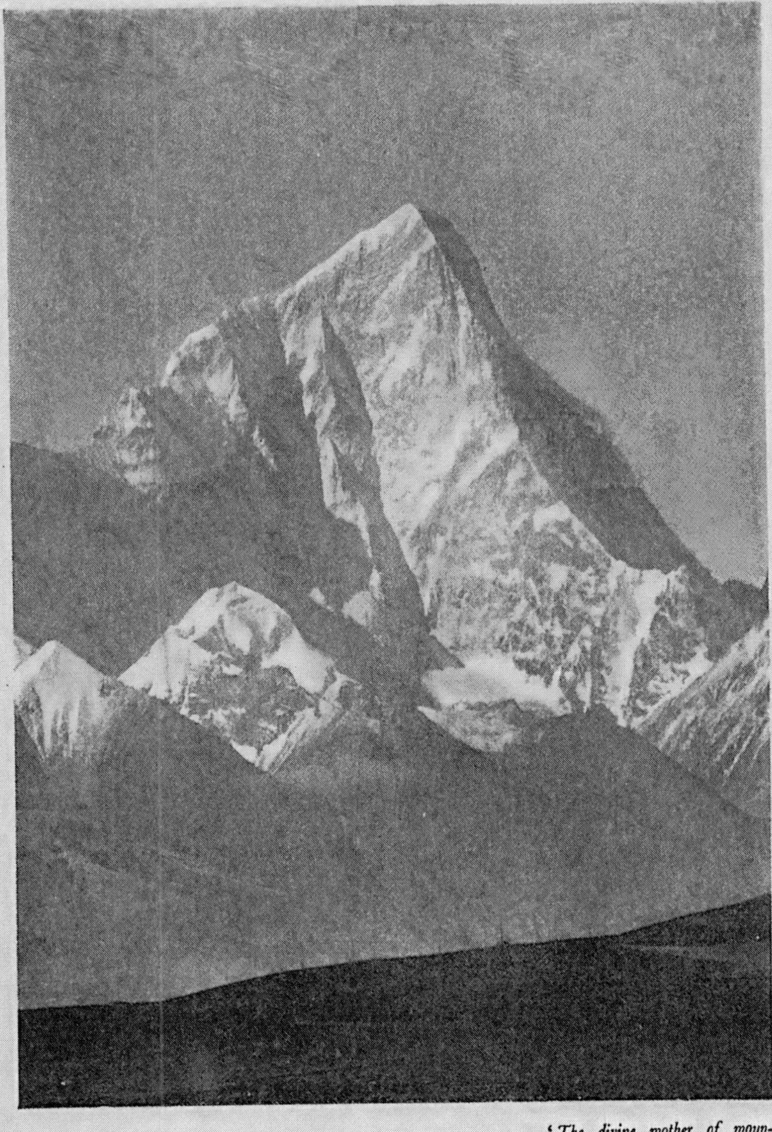

'The divine mother of mountains : unconquered, untrampled.'

the mountain side: soon Chumolaori sank out of sight. We were in Tibet.

Slush, mud, water, snow: we splashed through it all. We ran down the mountain side, jumped, slid, a medley of men, mules and ponies, until we reached the valley and that small broken causeway which marks the end of the road that men have built from Tibet to the foot of the Nathu La. Here we spoke once more, and words and speech that had seemed a meaningless mockery up above in the silence of the Pass, and gross disturbers of meditative rapture during the scramble down into the valley, became once more a medium of expression and an essential factor in our existence. We mounted our ponies and set off along the narrow path leading to Champithang—and the burden of our conversation and the clatter of our ponies' hoofs were—we are in Tibet.

The scramble down had been steeper and longer than had first appeared. The road leading to the foot of the Pass marked the snow line, and we found ourselves winding round the face of the hill on a steep path of soft sand. Soon vegetation returned in the shape of pine trees: not withered and blasted as if some fire had swept over them: but still bearing a stunted look. The trees became larger and thicker as we pressed on: the scenery resembled the woods in northern Germany at the end of a snow-fall in late January, when the thaw has left a dirty trampled coat of ice over the forest paths.

The road was a succession of loops, for all the world like some great sea-serpent that had left its ocean bed to creep along the mountain side. At the outside of the loops bearing away from the mountain the path overhung the valley and was free from snow: at the inside the loops brushed against sheer precipice, and the path was made up of pine logs thrown across horizontally, and built into the side of the mountain, covered with a thin layer of ice. The ponies were once more in their native country and knew it. They stepped out with great vigour, trotted round the outside loops and picked their way cleverly over the slippery logs; the air gradually filled with the scent of pine, and became warmer; we rode on in great spirits.

After some three miles we came to a clearing. The ponies broke into a canter, a sure sign that our destination was near at hand, and soon we saw a hut with chickens scratching in the muck-heap before it. A small hole had been cut into the side of it to serve as a window, and through the window was thrust the dirty face of a Tibetan woman. She yelled something to us, and pointed down the valley. We waved a welcome, cantered on and rounded the bend, where we saw, perched on a small hill to our left, the rest-house of Champithang.

It was built in the style of a Swiss châlet, of wood, with a long verandah and a small clearing in front shielded from the valley below by a wooden railing. We loosened our ponies' girths, tied them to the railing, and went into the bungalow.

The rooms were bare but large, with great fireplaces. A sniff on the verandah heralded the arrival of an extremely small boy with red and fat cheeks, staggering under the load of some great logs of wood. He threw them into the fireplace, announced with solemnity that he was the *chowkidar*, and ran for the fire. This he brought in a large shovel, and placed in the fireplace, for in Tibet the fire burns night and day all the year; then, going on his knees, in the intervals of his sniffs he blew the embers into flame, and soon had a large fire going. In spite of the fact that none of the smoke went up the chimney, but dashed back against our faces in a thick swirling cloud, the fire gave the place a decided air of warmth and comfort.

The boy himself was an interesting little creature. His father had died some twelve years previously and his mother, who was officially in charge, was an invalid, so that for some years he had been acting as *chowkidar*, and drawing the pay befitting that office, his only aid and abettor being a small dog with a curly tail. He was dressed in an English coat and breeches and a Balaclava helmet, with long Tibetan boots of red and blue wool and a thick muffler—for the most part garments that were relics of some old expedition. He looked after us well for all his sniffing, and, judging from the prices he tried to extort from us for fuel and oil, had a keen and practical mind for business. His oil, however, was bad and the lamps smoked abominably.

We had not to wait long for the servants, and opened a cake to celebrate the occasion, enjoying our tea as it has rarely been enjoyed before. We dipped into the three novels that comprised the bungalow library, and when these pathetic exiles had yielded their poor secrets, turned our thoughts and speculations to the new civilisation that was to be unfolded to us, or the old civilisation that was to be recalled, in the Chumbi Valley. The night drew on, dismally cold, heralded by the usual mist, which had swept over the Pass in our wake and had nearly caught us up before we reached Champithang. We transferred our fire from room to room, but all the chimneys smoked, so that we decided on the two inside rooms nearest the hillside as being more sheltered, and there we slept.

A hot bath in front of the fire before turning in made sleep a comfortable proposition, nor did the discovery that my British warm coat had been left behind at Changu tempt me to return for it.

V

THE CHUMBI VALLEY

WE woke to a brilliant sun and cloudless sky, and found to our delight that the bungalow of Champithang had been pitched among scenery even more beautiful than we had anticipated. From the bend of the valley we could see the ravine stretching up to the Nathu, with the pass clear cut and gleaming in the sun; strangely inaccessible it seemed, in fact our climb of yesterday appeared like a fantasy, a dream that had heralded this Swiss morning.

On the other side of the valley, which was about a mile across, towered the snow-clad buttress separating the approach to the Nathu from that to the Dzalep; great pine trees covered the lower slopes and filled the morning air with their scent. Far down in the opposite direction lay the Chumbi Valley and the road to Chumolaori.

My first care was for my British Warm, and I left a note to be handed to the next Tibetan wool train that might pass, so that the coat could be collected at Changu and taken through to the Doctor Sahib at Gangtok; all of which was done in this land of honest men, and the coat is with me now: but I was to feel the want of it badly later on.

We set off at eight o'clock on our ride to Yatung. The air was warm, all sense of bleakness had vanished, and one felt a great sense of comfort. The first bend in the road opened up Chumolaori and the majestic view of the snows stretching in a great arc from Chumolaori to the Nathu La, and for nearly two hours we marched with this vision before our eyes, until we came to Old Yatung, perched on the buttress that divides the valley of the Amo Chu. Southwards the river continued its way into Bhutan down a narrow valley, fertile and cultivated; north-east lay the Chumbi Valley, stretching to Phari.

Yatung has a curious history. It is the oldest of the four villages that form the Chumbi group—Yatung, Chumbi, Piphithang and Shashima—and, possibly on this account, had been fixed upon in the Treaty of 1893 as the place where the British should be entitled to have their Trade Agency. But the site was bleak in winter: wind howled round it, rain beat against it: a sheer drop of a thousand feet separated it from its neighbours. And yet the Treaty was made with great difficulty, and to alter it would be the work of kings. So they issue solemn edict. Shashima is no longer Shashima but Yatung, and Yatung is Old Yatung, and we will climb down from our perch and go to Yatung—the real Yatung—where we should have been all the time, for doesn't the Treaty distinctly state Yatung. So down the hill they go with great pomp and ceremony to the Yatung nestling so snugly in the valley, with its plain, and fields, and the pleasant waters of Amo Chu, in this fair strip of Tibet, and the Treaty is saved. By this simple exodus Simla and Lhasa rest in peace, and Old Yatung is left to its monastery and simple monks, perched high up away from impurity and anything likely to hamper meditation; but the men of Shashima are no more, and yet so perverse are they that they still call this Yatung of ours by

AMO CHU

'Continued its way into Bhutan down a narrow valley, fertile and cultivated.'

its old name, and Yatung, to them, is merely a monastery, where the lamas live and the prayer flags flap—*Om mane padme hum!*

The hill of Old Yatung is sandy, and on its summit stand three *chorten* overlooking the valley. These *chorten* are monuments to the dead and must be kept carefully on the right-hand side as a mark of respect. In Tibet proper, on the table-land, at such a place as Gyantse, the manner of disposing of the dead is a gruesome one. As a last act of devotion the dead man acquires merit by feeding the birds of the air and the beasts of the field with his corpse. The corpse is laid on a stone by the butcher—executioner and slaughterer in one: as near untouchable as the lower castes in India—and carefully dismembered and dissected in accordance with strict rites and ceremonies. The relatives of the dead man stand close at hand. Around huddle a group of vultures, in that unemotional state of expectancy which characterises the brutes. Farther off a pack of dogs snarling and growling, but keeping aloof from the feast out of regard for the dictates of precedence. The butcher picks up a kidney, or what you will, and solemnly names the recipient. The vulture flaps forward, takes the grim morsel, and flaps off to devour it in comfort—and so on with the rest of the flock.

When all the flesh and entrails have thus been portioned out the bones are broken up and distributed among the dogs. Hail to the jewel and the lotus!

The *chorten* were solidly built in Chinese style, and, being unacquainted at that time with Tibetan burial rites, we took them for the tombs of former abbots.

A short scramble down the hillside brought us to the Monastery. It was a large two-storeyed building, built of stone with red wooden roofs, surrounded by a thick belt of pine, looking very much like a large house of playing cards which nobody had had the indecency to blow down. We found but few lamas present: one who had once been a leper; another with the thickest and most heavily populated head of hair I have yet seen; and two small boys. They were dressed in long thick rusty-red robes of wool, and were all beams and smiles; at their invitation we passed through a gaily decorated archway into the courtyard.

The leper ran on in front and spun joyfully the large wooden spools with prayers painted upon them, which had been set in racks on each side of the gateway: but neither god nor man came out to welcome us.

The courtyard was empty, although the monastery was alleged to house 'nine times ten lamas,' for so the man with the hair expressed himself in his medley scraps of Hindustani. In the middle was a large stack of wood fuel, and into the north side cloisters had been built, decorated in red, yellow and blue, with scenes from the life of Buddha, and adorned with many fiends and ferocious beasts. Here the lamas are in the habit of sitting down in meditation, airing themselves in the sun—as well they might.

The lama with the hair showed the greatest interest in my camera, and insisted on looking through the sights as I took a snapshot of the courtyard. As a result his mop of hair not only brushed but rested against my cheek and neck for the best part of a minute—a distinctly unsavoury favour, nor did my imagination spare me as to the results of the caress.

The most interesting of the four was the smaller of the two boys: an urchin of eight years. In addition to his red cassock he had a peaked elf's cap of the same colour, and red and blue long woollen boots, while in a sack on his back he carried a skin containing holy water. As he was about to go down to Chumbi to visit his mother he offered to guide us into the village, and set off down the hill holding Bishop's hand. He answered Bishop's Hindustani, of which he understood nothing, with smiles and queer little Tibetan monosyllables, bounding and dancing along the path at a great pace, dragging Bishop down the hill in his wake. His elf's cap seemed to worry him, and after a while he took it off and laid it flat on the top of his head, and so balanced it.

The road swept round the hill in a wide detour, passing by great rocks and waterfalls, only lacking heather to be part of the Western Highlands of Scotland;, the sun-warmed haze was full of the hum of insect life, bringing to us both a general feeling of return to humanity. We were now close to the village, and, at a bend in the road, we saw our first yak, feeding by the wayside. Soon we came to a short cut, and Puck, as we had named him, pointed it out as the fitting and proper way to approach Chumbi. He then proceeded to go down it—to us it was a scramble, almost a climb—in what must be the orthodox way of taking short cuts to the good people of Shashima. He placed his hands rigidly by his sides, and by the simple process of stepping out into the air and allowing himself to fall until one of his feet lightly brushed the ground, when he at once thrust forward the other foot, descended in a series of bounds at an astounding pace. Having reached the bottom of some harrowing sector he would look back at the *sahiblog* in amazement, mingled with contempt, at their inability to imitate him. And so he proceeded, bounding forward in front of us like a will-o'-the-wisp, and gazing up reproachfully at our clumsy efforts to keep up with him; at last his patience gave way and, without even a wave of the hand, he broke into a trot which so exceeded anything we could accomplish that he was speedily lost to sight.

And so we came to Chumbi: a neat little village, with a very fine *chorten* at its approach upon which a gilded spire gleamed in the sun: we sat watching it from a mound above the village, until the syces arrived with the ponies.

The three villages in the Chumbi Valley are neat and clean to look at, and consist of large wooden houses, with wooden roofs in the form of planks, evenly cut, laid across the house and kept from blowing off by large stones. Between each village the land is cultivated, chiefly with barley, though the crops are meagre and of poor quality. The fields are small, and divided up by short stone walls, very much in the manner of Maltese cultivation. The streets in the village are narrow and winding, made up of great cobbles, with many twists and curves, just as if the houses had been built first and the paths to them had later become streets.

Two very fine large wooden houses facing each other, with a quaint gabled house forming the far side of the square, make the market-place at Chumbi; a yak train had just arrived, and the bales were lying on the ground in readiness to be despatched to India. The yak do not go further than Chumbi: thence onwards the wool is carried by mules over the passes to the Kalimpong bazaar; for the yak could not stand the heat of the Sikkimese valleys, and even the Tibetans themselves complain of the heat in Kalimpong and occasionally suffer from heat stroke.

This yak is a curious creature, a beast with long woolly nair, matted and thick as fleece: giant sheep and Highland cattle rolled into one. It is universal provider to the Tibetans, giving them its flesh for meat, its milk for butter, its hair for clothes, its tail for a whip, its dung for fuel and its own self for beast of burden and draught. It can go for long periods without food, and is at its happiest when snowed up, for in its natural state it lives in herds above the snow line; a hardy beast, well adapted to the barren bleakness of its haunts.

We rode through the winding streets, up over a bridge, and stopped at a small *ghuddi*—a house where one can get tea—by the wayside. The host was a cheery man with a smattering of Hindustani, doubtless a legacy from the Mount Everest Expedition. We were rather afraid of his tea, having heard much beforehand of this delicacy, which is a nauseating draught, food and drink in one, oily greasy food such as the cold man loves: yak butter and tea boiled up together, with a lump of mutton fat to float on the top if one is considered of sufficient importance to merit such a luxury. After a long canter on a cold day upon the table-land this tea becomes very refreshing if one has been long enough in the country to overcome its initial nastiness: we were never able to contemplate it with anything but horror, although Bishop was made to swallow several dishes of it before we returned to India.

We sat on the wooden form in front of the *ghuddi*, and looked about us, and returned the smiles of the small band of dirty happy Tibetans who had gathered around. We found that we were expected,—that sort of thing is not surprising in the East—and also heard for the first time mention of the 'lama sahib'—Dr. McGovern of the British Buddhist Mission—who had recently penetrated into Lhasa and was expected to reach the Chumbi Valley that night on his return journey. We had of course read of his achievement in Calcutta and knew that he was on his way back, but did not realise that our journey was so timed that we should meet at Yatung.

We found the group of villagers, which was steadily augmenting, rather oppressive, so we mounted our ponies and rode to the outskirts of the village, and sat on a large rock on the banks of the Amo Chu. Here we drank cocoa and munched biscuits, and watched two very small boys playing a Tibetan version of 'chuck halfpenny' in the river bed. They had scooped a small hole in the ground: from this they stood in turn about twelve feet away on a small rock in the water, and threw in succession a pebble, a small stone and a piece of rock into the hole. The scoring seemed complicated, but one boy was evidently more proficient than the other, for several coins passed his way when the game ended, and he strode away whistling like any schoolboy, leaving his disconsolate companion to practise diligently against a further encounter.

A few hundred yards away from Chumbi we were met by the British Trade Agent's son and with him we rode on to Yatung. The valley is not nearly as fertile as it appears from the heights above, and proved to be much narrower than we had expected. The Amo Chu, which tumbles down the middle, is a broad stream running rapidly through large rocks, and has every appearance of offering first class fishing. Actually the fish are very small and scarce, for the river is only a score of miles from its source and less than a dozen from the snow line.

We rode through the village of Piphithang. The road is straight and runs through the courtyard of the house of the Depön, the Chinese Trade Agent that was, who now acts as Tibetan Governor of this part of the world and has powers of life and death; we clattered past his courtyard unchallenged, for we had decided to postpone our visit to him until after our return from Phari.

Yatung itself—Shashima that was—is hidden from Piphithang by a bend north-eastwards; it is a large village divided into two parts by the Amo Chu. We were now on the right bank—having crossed by a large plank bridge beyond Piphithang—where lies the main part of the village, the Trade Agency, the Post Office, the guard-room for the platoon of the company forming the Trade Agent's escort—the main body is at Gyantse—and the polo ground, where Tibetan ponies are broken in and taught the tricks of their trade before being sent to India.

On the left bank, sheltered under the hill and commanding a sweeping view up and down the valley on either side, is the rest-house. To get to the left bank one crosses by a wooden arched bridge, so narrow and frail that ponies can only cross one at a time at a walk, and even after these precautions the bridge swayed ominously.

We galloped up the hill to the bungalow and took stock of ourselves and our surroundings. Our surroundings were very comfortable, ourselves less impressive. The bungalow contained a well-furnished dining-room, two comfortable bedrooms, and a verandah built in with glass and furnished with chairs and a large table. On our arrival this verandah was populated by a great number of formidable horseflies which had just awakened from their winter sleep and were emerging into life on this early spring morning. We slew some dozens with a fly whisk, covered the table with impedimenta, such as maps, whips, glasses, flasks, diaries, cameras and the like, and then solemnly took stock of ourselves. To say the least we looked dissipated. Our old faces had started to disappear and a new bright red face could be seen peering through the drifts of dirty dried skin that marked where the old faces had been. Some of the drifts were ready to shave off, but noses and cheeks were only in an elementary stage of peeling; indeed, Bishop's cheeks and nose were in such a condition that I contemplated putting a blue ribbon in his buttonhole before going to lunch at the Agency, lest our host might be induced to put a check on his hospitality in face of such a very obvious warning of what the consequences might be.

The Trade Agency is a picturesque house built on the hill overlooking the village, with a real garden where flowers and vegetables live and thrive. Here we found Mr. Macdonald and his family in their very comfortable home, and first enjoyed the hospitality which was to make our stay in Tibet so interesting and enjoyable. He has devoted the whole of his life to the study of Tibetan manners, customs, language

YATUNG

'Nestling so snugly in the valley, with its plain and fields, and the pleasant waters of the Amo Chu, in this fair strip of Tibet.'

and history, and every moment that we were with him we were more attracted by his knowledge and enthusiasm. In 1912, the year of the upheaval in Tibet that eventually led to the expulsion of the Chinese and the substitution of complete British influence, he was able to be of the greatest service to the Dalai Lama, a service which has resulted in a close friendship.

At the beginning of the upheaval the Chinese party had the upper hand and the Dalai Lama was compelled to fly from Lhasa. He started for the Chumbi valley with a small party of retainers and succeeded in reaching the Agency at Yatung a few hours before his pursuers, a band of Chinamen who were following him with orders to put him to death. Here he placed himself under the protection of Mr. Macdonald, who met the Chinamen at the gate and, after some negotiation, persuaded them to postpone their designs on the life of his illustrious guest and take up their quarters at the rest-house until the matter could be discussed with the ceremony and detail befitting such an occasion. And so the negotiations continued for some days, Mr. Macdonald riding backwards and forwards over the river each morning. By the time the negotiations had completely broken down and nothing but the fulfilment of their object would satisfy the Chinamen, he was able to tell them that the Dalai Lama had been smuggled over the passes in disguise into Sikkim, and was well on his way to Calcutta. That they did not choose him as a substitute was a compliment to the flag. They returned to Lhasa and no doubt joined the fugitives who fled northwards later when their nation was driven out of Tibet and their houses and villages were burnt to the ground, unless they had to bow to the executioner's sword for their failure to perform their task.

McGovern was expected in Yatung that night, and a tent had been pitched in readiness for him on the grass plot in front of the Agency. News came through later that he was spending the night at Goutsa and would arrive early the next morning, so that we calculated to pass him soon after we set out on our day's march.

The day passed very pleasantly. We lunched and dined at the Agency, talked a great deal, and listened more. For our host gave lavishly of his experience, and showed us his collection of the products of the country, including some very fine books and manuscripts. Tibetan methods of printing are primitive; the letters are carved out of wooden blocks, each block representing a page of the book. These blocks are kept by the printer himself on shelves, so that when a man would buy a book he must present himself at the printer's house, indicate the volume he requires, and either sit down and wait, or else go away until the copy is completed. The printer then collects the blocks for the book, and starts to produce a single copy, stamping the pages one by one, and returning the blocks to the shelves as finished. This system, as may be imagined, is not conducive to the best quality of workmanship, although it may be interesting as an example of the elimination of the middle-man. Well-printed books are very rare; although a popular pamphlet may be issued in large numbers the better and more important books are almost entirely found in manuscript, and Tibet is as medieval in this respect as it is in its castles, keeps, and mode of government: a country where monastic life forms the principal attraction of its inhabitants is not likely to progress, so that even now Tibet preserves in the fastnesses of the mountain plains of Central Asia a civilisation resembling closely that of England in the Middle Ages.

The manuscripts and books are written or printed on long narrow strips of thin tissue paper, oblong in shape, printed on both sides, and arranged to turn over from the bottom, so that they open like a concertina. They are carefully packed between ornamental boards, and tied with tape. The literary and publishing centre is Shigatse, the seat of the spiritual leader of Lamaism.

The principal subjects of the manuscripts are the lives of the Dalai Lamas, the history of the country, and certain obscure Buddhist philosophical treatises compared to which the works of Duns Scotus might have been written by Mr. Leacock. Of romance there is none, though one feels that surely an Amadis of Gaul once rode across those barren plains, clattered through the muddy towns, and caught a favour from the turret window of some Dzong as he passed. Possibly an epic may exist, hidden on the shelves of some printer or in the library of some monastery, and one day will see another great romance given to the world: in the meantime printer or librarian keep their treasures intact, and the monastery shelves are as dull as those of any college library.

We were shown many photographs of the country and the people, including a view of a corpse going through the process of acquiring merit, which spared no detail, even the *disjecta membra* in front of one overstuffed vulture being identifiable.

Two photographs showed a Chinese officer being executed for treason; in the first the expression of the victim's face as he waited for the sword to descend was that of intense interest in what was evidently going to be an important incident in his life and happy pride at being the subject of such an absorbing snapshot. In the second photograph the head had reached the ground—the executioner's sword had been very keen. There were also photographs showing the beginning of the proceedings usually adopted for driving the devils from a town, a ceremony that forms part of the New Year festivities. A man is chosen, usually by some marked physiognomical resemblance, to be the receptacle of all the demons and devils likely to harass the town during the coming year. He is dressed in suitable garb, and his features are made to look even more repulsive than Nature has contrived. As soon as the experts consider that his store of evil spirits has reached bursting point he is released with the whole town in hue and cry at his heels. Stones fly, staves are raised, swords, clubs, all are brought into play, and if he is overtaken he meets with short shrift. Sometimes he escapes with his life, and takes the devils from the village with him.

It is considered a sign of distinction to be chosen for the principal part in this comedy, and many a Nick Bottom strives for the honour.

In spite of this innate medievalism the Tibetans are not entirely lacking in enthusiasm for the attainment of knowledge. A small boy once presented himself at the Agency, weeping bitterly, and hugging a small peach tree under his arm. 'My father and mother are dead,' he explained, 'and I have nothing left but this peach tree. If you will look after me and send me to school I will give you this tree.' The boy is now on the way to be one of the brightest lights of the village of

Yatung that was Shashima, and the peach tree flourishes in the Agency compound.

At a late hour we crossed to the bungalow, preceded by a lantern, keeping a good look-out for dogs, for the Tibetan mastiff is very fierce and a force to be reckoned with at night when he prowls in packs. Save for a muffled snarl from the interior of a cottage above the bridge the village lay in silence.

VI

PHARI DZONG

To his intense relief we decided to leave the sweeper behind at Yatung. We found, however, that the syces were also reluctant to leave the valley, where they had found friends and refreshment, and the rumour that Gyantse was off his feed was chosen as the excuse to delay our departure. They had not reckoned with the veterinary attainments of Bishop, however, and the pony having been pronounced in good order we left Yatung at nine o'clock, driving them in front of us. The guard turned out and presented arms as we clattered by—a quaint reminiscence of the war and a wholesome reminder of the great Empire beyond the frontiers of which we were now riding.

The road was stony, and led up the side of a long narrow valley divided into sections by odd-shaped walls and little bastions of stone—sangars so called—forming a solid line of defence behind which a few well-trained marksmen could delay the advance of a considerable force. The remaining sections of the platoon of Rajputs who were supplying the guard at Yatung passed us on their way back from their morning drill and gave us a cheerful salute. The sergeant told us that the Lama Sahib was close behind, and at the next bend we met McGovern, walking a little way in front of his mules.

The impressions that we had previously formed of the leader of the British Buddhist Mission had been drawn entirely from the vague reports that had been published about him in the Calcutta newspapers, who had spared comment on his personal appearance. We had in mind a learned figure with a long black beard, arrayed in a black cassock with a soft black felt hat: almost certainly sitting on a white donkey and in all probability carrying a large umbrella. The sight of his tall, active figure, in ordinary raiment, full of energy and more than human, came as a great relief. We greeted him with enthusiasm, told him our plans, and arranged that he should wait for us in Yatung so that we could go back to Darjeeling together.

The details of his hazardous journey to Lhasa are now well known, but at that time his adventure was still a matter of speculation, and we were eager to be the first to hear the account of it.

We passed the villages of Gob Sorg—an old Chinese village with a keep overlooking the path, now deserted and ruined—and Galing Ka with its rickety bridge and straggling huts: then we turned by a bend overshadowed by rocks on which queer devils have been painted in red, and found the plain of Lingmathang stretched before us.

The plain is perfectly flat, and consists of a green carpet of short turf—closely resembling the turf of the Sussex downs—intersected by the many deviations of the Amo Chu. The plain is three miles long and at its broadest one mile across. It is completely enclosed by high wooded hills, almost perpendicular, painted in a riot of early spring colours, blues and reds with splashes of copper-coloured rock. Here we had our first canter, to the delight of the ponies, which had had more than enough of the scramble up paths of boulder and loose earth that had hitherto been their lot. We passed several yak trains carrying wool to Chumbi, and were entertained by the muleteers, who thrust out a red, swollen, lolling tongue by way of greeting. We persuaded four of them to stand for a photograph, one of whom was so reluctant that it was all his companions could do to make him stand in front of the camera. As soon as he heard the click of the shutter, he broke loose and dashed away with shouts and haloos, waving his arms in the air like a madman, thinking that a bullet must have passed through him or some evil spirit had gripped him by the hair. His companions chased after him in great glee.

We sat for some time in that quiet warm plain, a complete contrast to all that had gone before, and wished that the Chumbi Valley had been restored to Sikkim after the expedition of 1904; that Yatung had become a hill-station, and that it had fallen to our lot to be stationed in such a region. Shooting, fishing, riding, polo: Tibet and Bhutan with their unexplored fastnesses: a cheery people and no sedition: a place where a man could pass his life with all the glamour of an untackled job of work before him: a language comparatively unknown and a literature comparatively unread: possibly a treasure-house awaiting the explorer in the libraries of the great monasteries—there is a life's work in Tibet, but no man may devote his energies to it, and in that lies the tragedy. For the peace of the frontier it has been decreed that the country must remain inviolate, sacrosanct; here shall dwell men as they were, for ever; there shall be no Future, but always a Present, a Present that is the Past of other nations. And the wheels go on

GOB SORG

'An old Chinese village with a keep overhanging the path, now deserted and ruined.'

revolving the same prayers: the mendicant with his wheel, the lama with his wheel, the great monasteries with their wheels—the same prayers revolve again and again in a meaningless jingle of repetition.

Across the valley, where the river tumbles down from the plain, cloth and paper strips flutter the same prayers: up in the Passes, where the cairns mark the summit, the yak's tail waves the same prayers: in the gloom of the temple, where the shadows of the oil-lamps flicker across the calm golden features of the Buddha, the same prayers stir: in their small recesses the manuscripts lie wrapped in age-old dust. *Om mane padme hum !*

We left the plain and started to climb towards Goutsa. The scenery again changed; we found ourselves riding up a narrow gorge, with rock sides, purple and gold rocks, large trees with copper foliage, the Amo Chu a noisy torrent. The road was busy enough with a procession of yak trains taking the first consignment of wool since winter to Chumbi. Gyantse shied badly at one yak and scrambled up the hillside. The path was very narrow and passing yak trains became a slow and difficult undertaking.

We crossed to the right bank and found ourselves riding through a forest as beautiful as any we had seen in Sikkim. The road climbed steadily up, but opened as it went into a broad path with a grass track at the side, on which mules and yak were grazing contentedly. Owing to the prevalence at this time of the year in the upper passes of aconite in its early stages, which the animals are unable to distinguish from grass, mules and ponies are muzzled. The Goutsa gorge, however, seemed to be out of the zone of danger, for the muleteers made no effort to prevent their charges from grazing.

We passed several *ghuddis*, into all of which Gyantse expressed a strong desire to enter, and could only be withheld with the greatest difficulty, for he had a mouth of iron; in the end I adopted the principle of cantering as soon as we came in sight of a building. This was of no avail, for he displayed the same purpose, only on these occasions he was prepared to go through the door at a canter, so that I marvelled at the persistence of those who had ridden him in the past.

At length we came to a clearing where a new bridge of freshly felled pine had been thrown across the stream. There was a gate to the bridge over which a number of women were at work hauling logs to a large building in the process of construction on the opposite hill. Thinking we had reached our destination and that the gate to the bridge formed the entrance to the bungalow enclosure, and confirmed in our opinion by the action of the ponies, which automatically turned towards it, we rode through the gate. The women at once surrounded us and barred our path. We tried the words 'Goutsa' and 'Bungalow' but to no purpose. They stood by in amused astonishment. At length a woman called out something in Tibetan, and pointed further up the valley, whereupon, pursued by their derisive laughter, we turned back and continued up the valley, speculating as to the meaning of the large building on the hill, and the significance of the gate at the bridge.

We climbed for another mile until we came once more to a bleak and narrow ravine, at the head of which stood Goutsa, a small straggling hamlet of seven huts and a few prayer flags. The bungalow was the smallest we had yet found, but a fire and tea helped to add to its comfort. It was now about two o'clock in the afternoon, and the ravine was bleak and chilly. Just above the village the stream tumbled down some forty feet of rock with a steady comforting roar. We decided to make ourselves as comfortable as possible, and not stir out of doors again that day.

It was a restless evening. Bishop was not feeling fit at that altitude —Goutsa is over 12,000 feet high, too high for one who does not take kindly to sleeping at high altitudes—and would obviously feel better if he returned to Yatung instead of climbing still higher to Phari. So when I had pulled the last blanket about my shoulders I found many thoughts chasing away sleep: the question as to whether I should push on to Phari alone while Bishop returned to McGovern and waited for me was jostled out of court by the suspicion of a tickle in the middle of my back. I remembered all that I had heard of Tibetan encumbrances, those gelatinous, transparent beasts with hairy legs that nestle in the folds of one's shirt and prey on unresisting flesh. I racked my brains as to where we could get scarves for presentation to the Dzongpön in Phari, only to find that my suspicions of the slight tickle had become a certainty. I put out the light, and started to scratch, gently, soothingly, but monotonously, so that my eyes at length surrendered to sleep.

The next morning Bishop was definitely not well, so he returned to the Chumbi Valley while I pushed on to Phari. We decided that we would spend in Yatung the spare day that we had originally intended to spend together at Phari, when we had hoped to ride out over the

Tang La to Tuna. Our separation meant that Bishop would have three clear days in Yatung in the society of McGovern.

We divided up the caravan, Bishop taking one mule and his syce, and leaving the rest of our baggage with me. I found Gyantse strangely reluctant to leave Lucifer, and the first mile of the road was taken up in side-stepping, bolting up the hillside, and shying at most rocks. At length a stout switch cut from a wild peach put an end to the proceedings and the matter was settled.

The path led up by the torrent, then rose by a stiff climb to the hilltop, along a very awkward stretch of *khud*, ice covered and treacherous, so that Gyantse himself preferred to be led, until I came to a region bare of colour, life, sound, vegetation or even rock. A stretch of earth, plain brown soil, with barren lifeless hills on either side, cold and windswept, the last traces of the winter's snow thawing into the stream; a hot sun, a bleak wind, and absolute desolation. Across it, on tall poles, strangely sagging, a single telegraph wire, the wire to Lhasa.

A place bleaker than one can imagine; not dreary but senseless and sense-dumbing: a place to ride through in perplexity: another planet, or the return to earth after a gigantic flood; even the wire seemed mute, messageless. The plain opened out, became wider and flatter. As I cantered on, I tried to imagine it occupied, but could conjure up no being that could inhabit it. I passed a small group of kazis: they too seemed strangers to it, riding to get out of it. It stretched for nine miles. After six miles there was a sudden bend into a more enclosed plain, of brown mud, with a cup of hills around it: a brown sediment at the bottom of a cup three miles long. At the head of the cup lay the ugly medieval fortress of Phari: beyond the fortress, rising straight from the plain, lay the snow-white mountain Chumolaori.

A broad straight road stretched up to the fortress and Gyantse broke into a gallop. The exhilaration of the ride, the feeling of entering into a dream, of drifting back centuries, of dashing up to this grim old fortress at the foot of a fairy mountain, was the consummation of the journey. Fat tailless rats popped up from their burrows, blinked at the disturbers of their peace, and popped down again. The fortress came nearer and nearer, appeared more and more distinct: a long low wall lay like a screen before it; behind it a small monastery, perched on a mound. And so I came to Phari Dzong.

Through narrow, filthy streets, muck-littered; a dog's carcase trampled into the ground, soon to become part of the plain; dirty children, foul passages, mud-brick houses silted up so that they seemed dug into the ground; the Dzong wall, of stone, mud-cemented; all bore an indescribable impression of age.

Mists veiled Chumolaori, and a cold dank haze hung over the town, sending a shudder through me as I rode into the courtyard of the rest-house. The *chowkidar* had been servant to an officer in the Younghusband expedition and could speak Hindustani; with him as guide I walked back to the Dzong and sent salaams to the Dzongpön. We waited in a small dung-littered courtyard with the inevitable group of small children peeping round the doorway. At each side of the door were hanging great whips; near by stood a post ready for the offender.

The Dzongpön proved to be tall and sparely built. He was dressed in a long grey coat lined with blue silk, with an underskirt of black silk embroidered in gold. On his head he had a large brown bearskin hat. In his ears were turquoise rings, that in the right small and close-fitting, the left long and hanging down some five inches. According to the sages the man or woman who goes through life without his or her ears pierced is doomed to be reborn into the shape of a donkey, and as donkeys are common in Tibet it looks as if the lesson had still to be learnt.

He led me through several dark wooden passages and up some rickety stairs into a small dark room with low rafters, ill-lit and gloomy. A divan formed the only furniture, but a chair slightly higher than the divan was brought in for me. In Tibet it is the custom for rank to be signified by the height one sits from the ground. The guest takes a seat a little higher than the host: members of the household take seats a little lower than their master in accordance with their rank: menials sit on the floor. Of menials there seemed to be a number; I was aware of shadowy forms congregating in the gloom of the room, and whispering to one another on the floor; at my feet the *chowkidar* sat and acted as interpreter.

Conversation was difficult, for the Dzongpön spoke only Tibetan and Bhutanese, while my Hindustani is the poorest imaginable. We relapsed into signs, finally into beams and bows and faint sizzlings with the teeth that mark the bestowal of compliments. The dreaded tea was brought in, and I gulped as much of it as was consistent with an immovable countenance. A dish was set before me containing nuts and dried fruit, and certain unsavoury delicacies concerning which I feared to speculate. To my relief I found among them a bar of butter-scotch and a water-biscuit. The saving grace of the tea was the beauty of the cup in which it was served, an octagonal cup of fine porcelain, with saucer and lid: and the lid surmounted with a large turquoise.

After some fifteen minutes of fruitless attempts at conversation, the *chowkidar* came to my side, pulled my sleeve, and thrust into my hand a small fibre scarf which I handed over to the Dzongpön with great ceremony. He then conveyed to me that the Dzongpön was in the middle of important business and asked if I would like to see him at his work. On my agreeing my host smiled and led me into another room, almost the counterpart of the one we had left. Here a little below the divan a fat clerk with a very bald head was seated, writing with a wooden pen on a long screed of tissue paper folded concertinawise. On the floor was another clerk, counting out a heap of copper coins into little piles ranged in orderly rows. The scribe continued writing at the Dzongpön's dictation; he might have stepped from the company of Robin Hood, in girth and jovial mien a veritable Friar Tuck.

A chair had been brought for me, and I sat watching the scene with great interest. When the dictation was finished the Dzongpön read through carefully what had been written and made several alterations; evidently some tax or contribution was about to be sent to Lhasa.

I watched for some time, then took my leave and climbed on to the roof of the Dzong with the *chowkidar*. The actual fortress was completely dismantled by the Younghusband Expedition, and the ruins are still lying just as they had been left when the British sappers had finished with them. It was significant of the barrenness of the Phari plain that not the slightest sign of overgrowth was visible.

I climbed down to the town and took some twenty photographs of various kinds, all of which promised to be most interesting. Unfortunately the afternoon was so gloomy and my knowledge of photography so limited that they were largely failures.

The town proved dirtier and more noisome than I had imagined. A large earth wall had been built across the plain as a wind-screen, and behind this were huddled groups of mules, ponies, dogs, and yak. As soon as a mule had been released from his burden, or a pony from his master, the beasts went of their own accord, unheeded, to the wall and joined the group sheltered behind it. When their owner had finished his business he strode over to the wall, collected his mules, pony and dog and continued on his way.

Phari is close to the Bhutanese frontier, the nearest Bhutanese town being only some two miles distant; in consequence it is the centre for all the trade going both from India and Tibet into Bhutan, and is a most important market. In addition to the mule trains there are two-wheeled carts, drawn by bullocks or yak, which carry the bulk of the trade, and for decoration have a tall bamboo pole with prayers flapping from the end of it.

The Dzong therefore had held and guarded a most important point, controlling the trade of three countries; and Phari, but for its bleakness, would be a much more suitable site for a Trade Agency than Yatung. The Phari plain is also an integral part of that portion of Sikkim which the giant finger once clawed into Tibet, for it is six miles south of the Great Himalaya Range, which is crossed at the Tang La, at the foot of Chumolaori. Our influence, however, stretches fifty miles

PHARI DZONG

'Surely an Amadis of Gaul once rode across those barren plains, clattered through the muddy towns, and caught a favour from a turret window as he passed.'

beyond the Pass to Gyantse, where the remaining three platoons of the company forming the Trade Agent's escort are stationed. By this disposition of our forces, then, we are able to combine defence against a sudden movement towards India, the control of the important mart at Phari, and the amenities of life in the Chumbi Valley.

The Bungalow and the British Post Office stand side by side in a rectangular courtyard sheltered by a high wall. The rooms of the Bungalow were small and the chimneys smoked abominably: however, I was fortunate enough to find wood fuel and not yak dung burning in the hearth. The servants arrived some time later, and I had just started tiffin when the Dzongpön came to return my visit.

I found my position as host more difficult than that of guest. Deeming him possibly to have some smattering of military education I showed him my maps, but they evidently conveyed nothing to him, so I plied him with marching-chocolate and tea. He then turned his attention to my personal belongings: tried on my gloves, opened my camera and exposed a film, and finally seized my thermos flask. I had been forewarned that he had a habit of hinting for the gift of anything that attracted his attention so that I was prepared for that eventuality. The fact that the contents of the flask were hot aroused great curiosity in him, and when I told him that the cocoa had been made for over eight hours he certainly took me for a liar or a miracle-monger.

I was very hungry, but he showed no signs of departing, so I continued eating while he sat and watched me. Suddenly he clapped his hands and a small boy appeared with a basket of eggs and the identical scarf handed to me by the *chowkidar* during my visit to the Dzong. This the Dzongpön placed round my neck for some unaccountable reason, seeing that it is the usual custom to hand the scarf with a bow, and resumed his seat. I handed him my cigarettes and he took three; as supplies were short, it was essential to get rid of him, and I was at a loss until Tchugro the bearer, in a moment of inspiration, produced the brandy and half filled a couple of glasses. While I was groping for the water the Dzongpön swallowed the neat brandy and went off into a fit of choking and spluttering. When he had recovered I suggested a little water, and as soon as the drink was finished he rose to go. He asked if I would dine with him that night, adding that he had several old Tibetan things to show me, but as a Tibetan dinner is an elaborate affair of many doubtful courses and I had no wish to add to my pack a lot of worthless curios sent from Calcutta for the purpose, I pleaded fatigue and need of sleep: and so he went, with a cheery wave of the hand and possibly a poor opinion of my worth. I handed back the scarf to the *chowkidar*, who put it in his pocket for further use.

I heard later that I was wise not to go, for the Dzongpön is famous for getting the best of a bargain. There is a bird that inhabits the table-land of Tibet and lays a very small egg of turquoise blue. This egg when frozen has the appearance of a precious stone, and is sold as a curiosity for a couple of tronkas, about sixpence in English money. A stranger riding through Phari once called on the Dzongpön, who, according to custom, started admiring the personal belongings of his visitor, especially his Webley revolver; at length he asked him if he would sell it. The stranger said that he did not wish to part with it, but he would let the Dzongpön have it for two hundred and fifty rupees.

The Dzongpön replied that he would give in exchange for it a precious stone worth more than the sum named, and sent a servant to fetch the jewel. When the stranger saw the jewel, which was in a small casket, he said: 'Excellent, I have its counterpart,' and drew from his pocket one of these frozen eggs. 'In fact,' he continued, 'if anything, mine is of slightly better finish, and I bought it near Everest for two tronkas.' The revolver did not change hands.

I was wise also not to dine with him, for Tibetan hospitality implies a familiar interest in the welfare of the guest's appetite. As a mark of honour a man will take a choice morsel off his own plate and place it in his guest's mouth with his own chopsticks—and after some half dozen courses those chopsticks, which have been retained from dish to dish, have ceased to be attractive.

As soon as the Dzongpön had gone away I went into the Post Office and found a typical babu post-master, sitting solemnly down before his receiver and writing out a report of a political speech made in London the day previously. I asked him for some stamps but, to my surprise, he told me he could not let me have any for half an hour as it was Sunday and he was not open until half-past four. He was full of woes and 'big begs' and had all the diction of the Bengali babu at his command. He explained that he was a Sikkimese from Gnatong who had been educated in Calcutta and had been sent to Phari as a punishment. He hoped to return to Gnatong as soon as his deputy, who was at Lhasa, had been trained sufficiently to relieve him. He had been in Phari nine months and did not consider Tibet a 'convenient place for a gentleman.'

This conversation occupied half an hour, and as the clock hands reached half-past four he sold me two stamps and took down a telegram, the first commercial transaction that had come his way for six months. Some minutes later the parcel post arrived from India, and I was surprised at its size and the number of its packages.

The night was bitterly cold and the fire smoked incessantly. I tried to read *Joseph Vance*, but the irritation to my eyes from the smoke drove me to bed, so I piled every available garment on the top of me, and greatly lamenting the absence of my British Warm, fell to sleep.

VII

THE GOUTSA GORGE

I WAS awakened by the *chowkidar*, who put his head through the door and bellowed the one word 'Chumolaori' as if he were the guard of some dream train. The mountain was visible from the window of the next room, and I was saved a trek in pyjamas and gum boots to the exterior of the bungalow. It seemed so near that a stone could be tossed on to it; to climb it seemed the task of an hour—Cruachan piled on Cruachan. Every crevice and crack glittered in the sun; sharp peak and knife back, rising straight up from the brown plain.

I weighed the question of pushing on over the Tang La to Tuna, and decided to abandon the plan, seeing that it would possibly prevent me returning to Yatung on the next day as promised; so I consoled myself with a large breakfast and prepared to leave Phari.

The muleteer was Phari-born, and Tchugro and the syces were prepared to celebrate his return to his native town for another twenty-four hours, so a string of excuses was reeled out, with a touching picture of a fast failing Gyantse to give strength to the arguments; but all to no purpose.

I set out from Phari with great reluctance, and so did Gyantse, who was fully determined to visit the town of his birth from which he had taken his name, some eighty miles beyond the Pass: deeming his case a hard one, brought thus to the edge of his native land, allowed to peer into it and then to be rudely driven away: when the air was clear and invigorating: no mist, no cold, only the beauty of the mountain sparkling in the morning sun: Tang La but half a dozen miles distant, promising a glimpse of the plain beyond the Great Range.

So we fought it out all the way, trotting sullenly here, turning with a rush and galloping to the rear: given our head, pulled up with a jerk and turned again: a sudden trot, another turn, another gallop: another twist and our head turned to Goutsa: the whole of Phari plain for our manoeuvres. Defiance: refusal to budge: a beating: so we continued until the bend was reached and the Dzong and mountain had receded behind the hill; then a steady canter towards Goutsa and the struggle was over.

With the end of the plateau Tibet ends, for Phari is Tibet and to see Phari is to see the whole of Tibet save its great cities. There are two small plains after the descent from the plateau, and over the mountain side of the first of them hangs a notable waterfall, the frozen fall at Dotah. This was the outpost of the land of desolation.

We gradually returned to life. First the Amo Chu bubbled and chattered as its many threads were gathered into one skein, tumbling over the boulders in ecstasy at the thought of life and human habitation in front of it. Then the hills showed touches of colour, early morning colour. Stunted pines appeared and a few rhododendron shrubs, their sticks peering out of the snowdrifts: finally straggling bushes, their pink tips proclaiming where the first leaves would unfold.

GOUTSA GORGE

Bubbled and chattered as its many threads were gathered into one skein.'

There were now no mules to pass, for the empty trains had not yet had time to reach the Goutsa gorge on their return from India. I caught up one train on its way to Chumbi and rode with it for some time, the road being too bad to proceed at anything faster than a walk. The sun had had a short life and mist and rain were threatening, so that I was glad that I had not made for Tuna, since the journey would have been bleak and cold and the plains beyond hidden in mist.

I reached Goutsa early. The sun had held just long enough for me to get clear of the plateau; the last few miles were grey and cheerless, and it had started to rain before I reached the bungalow. From the window I watched the wool trains winding through the village. On our journey up from Chumbi we had met yak trains; to-day the wool was being carried by mules. As one of these mule trains came through the village a small pig attached himself to the caravan, possibly with the idea of seeing it safely across the few planks that formed the bridge across the stream. As the last mule crossed, the pig turned back and found to his dismay that the muleteer, a swashbuckling young fellow with a stone in his hand, stood between him and home. He swerved like a three-quarter, dodged the stone and did the fastest hundred home that I have seen for some time.

Three hours later the mules and servants arrived. Seeing that the grey mule had gone back to Yatung with Bishop, the miserable specimen had carried my valise and the food box all the way to Phari and back, a most unequal share of labour, for the others had practically nothing. They came through the village in their usual order. First the old mule, acknowledged leader, weighed down with a small kit-bag and a pair of boots. Then Mule No. 2, loaded with bells, a bag of fodder and the bread box. Some ten yards in the rear, staggering under his great burden, came the miserable specimen. The two leading mules, deeming that Yatung was our goal, overshot the mark and crossed the plank bridge with the muleteer in hot pursuit. All this was observed by the miserable specimen who, possibly warned by the pig, turned aside at the right place and lopped up the approach to the bungalow. The other two, headed back by the muleteer, dashed along in his wake. So they came up, a mass and jumble of baggage, legs and bells: the old mule striving to regain his lead: the second mule determined to snatch at last the old mule's privilege: the miserable specimen filled with a desire to put both of them in their places—and he won, by a neck it is true, but an undoubted victory. There was triumph in the twitch of his tail as he settled down to the smallest and lightest nosebag.

Goutsa is bleak and desolate: the wind buffets against the bungalow: the Amo Chu roars at the opening of the gorge. I piled on clothing, opened a new cake and sampled some of the Dzongpön's eggs. They were very old, some of them more than three or four years: some of them even refused to fry, which implies senility in a Tibetan egg, and were mercifully dealt with by Tchugro. Of the basketful some half dozen were reported to me as eatable and were eaten: Tchugro and his friends probably accounted for another dozen: so that half were thrown away.

Food is not a delicacy in Tibet: it claims veneration rather than respect. There is mutton to be had in the valleys where the sheep can find pasture, but on the table-land they eat chiefly old frozen yak, kept for some years to mature, freezing at night, just not thawing at midday, in a state of suspended decomposition, tough and stringy and blackened, sometimes smoked with yak dung: old eggs that collapse in time or are destroyed: and yak butter, cut into squares and frozen solid like blocks of clouded amber, handy as a missile, but more usually cooked in tea as the chief offender in the staple diet of the country. Into the great houses penetrate unearthly eatables, dried fruits, juiceless and musty, which have found their way down through Tibet from China: and side by side with them, heaped in a great dish, stale chocolates and biscuits brought years since from Kalimpong. And with his long claw-like nail, unwashed, the kazi gropes through these delicacies, so often handled, rakes out the least appetising and offers it to the guest.

For drink there is *chang*, a light and harmless barley beer: *malwa*, a spirit such as the peasant loves: and pure alcohol, sour and sickly, yet potent, with a ritual for drinking that is known from China to Russia by way of Turkestan.

In addition to the eggs I had also brought a scarf from Phari which carried the whole smell of Phari in its folds: a mixed fragrance of yak and butter and tea and dirt. These scarves are made of a coarse fibre and are reduced to pulp if they get wet. To important people, such as the Depön, or the Abbot of a large monastery, it is the custom to present a fine silk scarf of a gay colour; in ordinary life and when dealing with minor officials, such as the Dzongpön, who is petty magistrate and customs official in one, a fibre scarf serves the purpose.

I sat before the fire in the ill-lit room and read on until the last log had burnt through, when I went to the door of the bungalow and peered out. It was a clear night, but no moon: a few stars gleamed in the sky above the gorge: the huts that formed the hamlet were in darkness. From the servants' hut shone the light of a large fire, and the rise and fall of a voice betrayed Tchugro, in the middle of an account of some of his adventures in those famous days when he had set out to climb Everest.

I left Goutsa at half-past eight the next morning, and set off for Yatung in a calm and leisurely fashion. The gorge was at its finest, and was even more beautiful to descend than it had been to climb. At one point it opened out into a circular cup, of which the diameter was so narrow that one had the impression of being at the bottom of a cylinder. The sides of the cylinder were pine-covered, streams tumbled down the slopes and mingled with the torrent of the Amo Chu; peering over the brim of the cylinder, like a giant child peeping into a box of silkworms, the snow-capped crest of a mountain.

The road descended by a steep decline round the sides of the cup: the air was warm and fragrant: the vegetation luxuriant, akin to the warm sheltered valleys in Sikkim: a carpet of leaf-mould covered the path. I heard the jingle of bells across the cup and saw approaching a caravan more pretentious that any I had previously passed.

A servant rode in front on a white pony with red and blue trappings: behind him came another retainer; then an individual with an air of much importance in Chinese dress, wearing a pigtail. He was dressed in a long silk overmantle reaching to his stirrups, and had a circular hat with a tassel; a pair of large spectacles added to his dignity. He raised his whip solemnly in greeting and passed on, followed by a small group of servants mounted on mules. I heard later that he was an official from Lhasa who had been sent to prospect for a site suitable for the building of a mint. His choice had finally fallen on the gorge at Goutsa, and the new building that had engaged our attention on our way up was the result of his mission; this explained the reason for the gate at the bridge from which we had been so unceremoniously hustled. It is to be hoped that the coins minted there may rival in workmanship the beauty of their surroundings.

Tibetan money has a romantic appearance, but that is the most that one can say for it. The standard coin is the *Tronka* (the 'r' in this word is not pronounced); of thin beaten silver, a little smaller than a florin, stamped on one side with a central floral design surrounded by eight ovals containing Tibetan characters; on the reverse the ovals are replaced by flowers. It is worth three annas of Indian money, or approximately threepence. The lower values are copper, and the greater part of Tibetan trade is carried out in copper values. The sum of money that was being counted before the Dzongpön was made up entirely in copper; fines and bribes are calculated in copper.

The lowest coin in value is the *Kakang*: one-sixth of a tronka. It is round, smaller than a shilling, and has as its central design a four-footed animal with six wisps of tail and six tresses of beard. Whether this represented a snow leopard, a devil, or a yak I was unable to discover, but the beast appears on all the copper coins.

The next coin in value is the *Karmanga*, equal to one-third of a tronka. As this coin has twice the value of a kakang it was for some time double its size. Such a state of affairs is fraught with difficulty for an illogical mind, so a new coin has been introduced half the size and half the weight of a kakang. So that there are two karmangas, one four times the size and weight of the other, and yet of the same value: one half the size of its half and a quarter the size of its equal: which makes calculation confusing to the stranger.

The *Chegye* comes next—half the value of the tronka, a coin intended to be shaped like the Indian anna—a rose. The Chegye is rare, and it is fashionable to bite, hack, or chew a piece out of a tronka to act in its stead. If you are able to make three chegyes out of one tronka, so much to your advantage. A piece so hacked should contain four ovals from the border in order to be negotiable, but hard use wears away the design, and a small silver fish-like thing usually passes muster.

The highest in value of the copper coins is the *Shokang*, equal to two-thirds of a tronka. Its outstanding feature is the fact that its edges are milled: otherwise it is identical in size, weight and appearance with the kakang, which is only a quarter of its value. There are three gold coins, the Shonga, Ngusang and Sertrang, worth 3⅓, 6⅔, and 133⅓ tronkas respectively. It is not surprising that there is argument in the market-place when a man attempts to give change for a Sertrang in karmangas against a bill for fifty-nine-and-a-half tronkas. It is an interesting coincidence that the supracargoes of the East India Company were put to a similar mathematical test when they began to open up trade with Canton. The Chinese measures of weight are the tael, the catty and the picul. Sixteen taels go to make one catty and one hundred catties make a picul. Unfortunately the equivalent of one tael in avoirdupois was $1\frac{1}{3}$ ounces, so that the conversion table read—

$$1\tfrac{1}{3}\text{ oz.} = 1\text{ tael,}$$

$$1\tfrac{1}{3}\text{ lb.} = 1\text{ catty,}$$

$$133\tfrac{1}{3}\text{ lb.} = 1\text{ picul,}$$

and with this encouragement they set out to barter in pidgin English with the most astute race of the world, whose previous experience of Europeans had been confined to the Dutch.

I reached the plain of Lingmathang without further incident, clambered down the road from Galing Ka to Gob Sorg, and trotted on to Yatung. I found the sweeper, stark naked, stripped even of his loin-cloth, whirling round in a fantastic dance on the lawn in front of the bungalow, to the huge delight of the *chowkidar* and the syce, who beat the rhythm with their hands, and the intense interest and gratification of a number of Tibetan ladies, who had left their work to view the spectacle. On seeing me he stopped his dance, hastily wound his *pugaree* round his head and gave me such a boisterous welcome as to proclaim that he had found ample consolation for his past sufferings in the native *malwa*, of which he had somehow contrived to obtain large quantities. The syce, as he held Gyantse's head and loosened his girths, poured out to me a long story of mules and Lucifer and baggage, of which I understood very little but took to be an announcement of Bishop's safe arrival from Goutsa two days before. On my expressing great satisfaction he seemed somewhat surprised, and with good reason, as I realised when I heard the full burden of his tale. On the way down the grey mule had taken fright and bolted, pursued by Bishop on

Lucifer. During his flight the girths holding the baggage had loosened with the shock of the boxes bumping against boulders: the medicine chest had broken open and some two miles of the Goutsa gorge were strewn with minute bottles of drugs, poisons and medical paraphernalia of all kinds. The mule was caught and tethered and some time was spent in retracing their steps and gathering as much of the contents as could be found. There were, however, several bottles still missing and the stuff inside some of these was such as to cause considerable anxiety to the medical mind, which had visions of peasants and muleteers picking up tiny bottles on the road as they passed and stopping to sample the contents. It seemed barely possible that the miserable specimen of mule could let such an opportunity slide, but he turned up in good enough style, and if he had a bottle of ipecacuanha inside him he carried it like a man.

Finding that Bishop and McGovern had gone for a walk, I rode over to the Trade Agency, where I was regaled with cakes and tea and heard that my companions had walked up the valley to meet me. On their return they insisted that they had not left the road the whole way, and as it was impossible for me to do so on Gyantse the fact that we had missed one another remained a mystery, unless they had been so engrossed in philosophic controversy that they had been changed into wraiths by some passing bogey, and rendered invisible. Possibly the demons of Tibet, in revenge for the violation of their sanctity, had filled Bishop with medicine stranger than any he had left behind in the Goutsa gorge, or had converted McGovern into the little old man who had passed me near the fort at Gob Sorg, staggering under the weight of

LINGMATHANG

'A green carpet of short turf, intersected by the many deviations of Amo Chu.'

a great pack of wool. For it was in this way that McGovern had travelled the greater part of the road to Lhasa, disguised as a Tibetan coolie, with half a maund on his back: his eyelids gummed down with mucilage to prevent the discovery of his blue eyes and give the illusion of snow-blindness: a straggling beard in early growth of which he would be immensely proud, for a beard is a great honour among Mongol races and falls to the lot of few men to cultivate. Indeed, enquiries about the beard were not the least awkward problems that he had to face, and the Sikkimese ancestry which was put forward as an excuse for his accent served also for an excuse for the reddish fringe which threatened daily to straggle less and bush more in accordance with the Western habits of beards.

Bishop returned to the bungalow in time for tiffin, and from him I heard of the mishap to the mule. By the time we had related our adventures the afternoon mist had drawn on, taking the form of a light drizzling rain; the temperature, which had been at 70° at midday, dropped very suddenly to 50°, and it became increasingly colder as the afternoon wore on. Sweaters were donned, more logs heaped on the fire and Bishop, carefully prescribing a bottle of bullseyes as a convenient gag for me in such conditions, for my pipe had lost its savour, wrote letters undisturbed while I finished *Joseph Vance*. After some discussion in the failing light we picked out each his least soiled collar and, thus embellished, we walked over to the Agency for dinner.

We found a very comfortable party feverishly engaged in the pursuit of 'Coon Can' and added ourselves to the number. A cheerful evening followed, in the course of which we elicited a lot of information from McGovern as to his adventures.

He had reached Lhasa at the beginning of the New Year Festival, the great event in the Buddhist calendar, which is held early in February. The monks from the great monasteries make pilgrimages to Lhasa in order to share in the festivities, so that the greater part of the population of the country is collected in the capital city for the three weeks of the festival. In consequence the streets are thronged, lodgings are unavailable, and men camp in ditches and under walls and wherever shelter can be found, and it was only after much ado that he could find shelter without revealing himself. When news of his arrival had been circulated among the people, an infuriated crowd of lamas assembled outside his lodgings, resolved to tear in pieces the foreign devil who had come against the will of his own government and for whose death his government would take no action, for so the matter appeared to the Tibetan mind. Songs of hate and martial cries and gnashing of teeth were added to the popular rejoicings, and soldiers were sent to protect him; for in Tibet there are two parties, a new political situation due to circumstances arising from the expulsion of the Chinese.

The government of Tibet is carried on by the Dalai Lama, who, as temporal head of the State, has absolute powers. Under him are four Shapes, viziers who are responsible for the government of the country. When the Dalai Lama returned from Calcutta to Lhasa to resume the government of his country he had British encouragement and influence behind him, and without that influence he would have had a hard task to regain his position. This he did, and instituted a Liberal government friendly to the British and determined to prevent the re-establishment of Chinese influence. He was chiefly supported by one Shape, Tsarong, the Commander-in-Chief of the Army, an extremely able and honest man, with great strength of character. With British support this party has governed Tibet ever since, in spite of the fact that it is very much in the minority.

The majority comprises the abbots of the great monasteries, the monks, and other religious bodies who, being strictly Conservative, look on their old masters the Chinese as their natural friends, since their religious customs and in a sense their language are the legacy of Chinese occupation or suzerainty. They represent approximately forty per cent. of the population, and are firmly against development or anything likely to disturb the placid existence in the monastery that they have enjoyed so long. In consequence they view with alarm certain progressive measures that have occurred recently in Tibet through British influence, such as the linking up of Lhasa to India by telegraph, and the equipping of an army with guns and modern rifles, so that it shall be sufficiently strong to defend the northern frontier against any Chinese invasion. In the present disturbed state of China this eventuality is not to be taken seriously, for a Chinese general commanding an expeditionary force sufficiently large to conquer Tibet would not proceed many miles before the prospect of using it more profitably in the present civil strife would appear far more attractive; at least it is a point of view that would suggest itself in Pekin before such an expedition would be sanctioned—and good soldiers are now at a premium.

Even the Dalai Lama himself is in a position of great personal insecurity, for he is the first in succession to be a ruler and not a figure-head, and in a sense has usurped the power which originally lay with the Tibetan nobility, from whom the Shapes are drawn. In the past it was the custom to poison the Dalai Lama at the age of eighteen; the incarnation passed into a peasant child of about six years who was elevated to the throne, and the country was governed by the nobility on such terms that no jealousy could arise on account of the supreme power resting with any one particular family. The present Dalai Lama was preserved from death by the Buriat Dorjieff, who was living in Lhasa ostensibly as a Buddhist priest at the time of the Younghusband Expedition in 1904, although actually he was a Russian Agent, and as such the prime cause of the Expedition. It was possibly with the idea of controlling the supreme power that he worked to preserve the life of the Dalai Lama, and carried him off northwards on the approach of the British.

Although Russian influence vanished as a result of Colonel Younghusband's mission, the Dalai Lama returned and took over the government of the country into his own hands. In consequence, with the exception of the Commander-in-Chief, the nobility tend to alienate themselves from the Liberal party and closely ally themselves with the monastic party. British friendship, therefore, is an essential factor to the continuation of the power of the Liberal party and a progressive policy in Tibet. The Dalai Lama himself is closely guarded and his food is tasted very thoroughly before it is set before him. The death either of him or of his powerful minister, Tsarong, would create a difficult position in Tibetan politics.

The arrival of McGovern then, contrary to the wishes of the British Government, seemed to the more fanatical element in the Conservative party an excellent opportunity to pull a Britisher to pieces, while the one thing which the party in power were anxious to prevent was any cause of unpleasantness with the British Government. So the monks howled outside the door while McGovern escaped by the roof and photographed them unobserved with his cinematograph camera.

VIII

YATUNG, OR SHASHIMA

THERE being no need to rise early I lay peaceably in bed on the next morning and through the open door watched Bishop dress an abscess on a pony's neck. The pony was a rough, bedraggled beast that had been recently purchased from a mule train. It was difficult to realise that after four months' training and a good clipping he would appear as smart and active as Lucifer; for the Bhutia has an appearance of neat clean energy all his own, eager for work and brimming over with vitality. The dressing finished, I had no further excuse to remain in my bed, so I shaved off another layer of face, the Phari layer, and went to breakfast. We had arranged to call on the Depön that morning and, as we did not wish to go through the ceremony of lunching with him, Mr. Macdonald gave us an excuse by inviting us to a Tibetan lunch at the Agency, to be eaten with chopsticks in the approved fashion. There was another reason for not lunching with the Depön; some days before a Chinaman had been arrested for insulting behaviour in the bazaar and, since no punishment had yet been meted out to him, it was considered unadvisable for the Depön to be fortified by the potations inseparable from the entertainment of guests to a tiffin of some twenty courses, in case he might wish to amuse himself subsequently at the hapless Chinaman's expense. So, strongly admonished to be a restraining influence in this matter of liquor, we rode down the valley along the banks of the Amo Chu to Piphithang. McGovern did not accompany us, for part of his journey to Lhasa had been made through territory under the jurisdiction of the Depön, and he was not held in great favour on that account.

The outer courtyard of the house of the Depön has been built in the middle of the village itself. The main cobbled street runs through the courtyard and can be closed at either end by gates; at each of the gates, which are built into a large wooden wall, there is a broad step over which the ponies picked their way. The main doorway has a flight of six long narrow steps leading up to it, and is flanked by two wooden columns, carved in Chinese fashion and picked out in colours, supporting a heavy architrave of carved wood.

At the doorway stands a whipping post. Heavy thonged whips hang from the wall, and close at hand are chains and other devices the uses of which were explained to us; one of these provided a barbarous method of administering justice. It consisted of a square of wood with a circular aperture cut out of the middle. The delinquent is stripped, doubled up and trussed like a fowl: the aperture is forced over his hindmost quarters and that part of his anatomy thus exposed is smacked slowly into a raw pulp with a flat baton four inches wide, not unlike a harlequin's wand.

Tibetan methods of punishment are very grim. Until recently mutilation had been the usual medium for administering justice, very much on the lines of early Mediaeval England; a thief lost a left hand for his first offence, and a foot for a second. The executioner's knife was keen and the wound was seared with a burning brand; the shock of the blow would be to the criminal's advantage, and by the time he had recovered his senses the worst would be over. To be whipped to death is a tedious process, and the victim suffers much before his senses mercifully leave him. Of the blows that follow till life has left his body, of the blows rained on the quivering flesh until the sentence has been fulfilled, he knows nothing.

In the great cities, where the administration of justice is placed in the hands of a body of men specially deputed for that purpose, stripes have a commercial value, so that a man may buy off a lash for a karmanga, and a fee to the executioner will ensure gentle dealing. A man sentenced to one hundred and fifty lashes, which is well beyond the death margin, may buy half of them from the judge, compound with the executioner, and receive ten of the best only. But for the man with no karmangas such a sentence offers no hope but a mule and grappling hooks to drag his remains from the market-place.

Beyond the main doorway is a small enclosed courtyard, with shrubs in pots and a patch of grass, facing the house. The main room was large and dirty, an ordinary room with bare walls and wooden floor, lighted by large windows and lacking altogether the romantic atmosphere of the rooms in Phari Dzong, with their low ceilings and large beams, full of black shadowy recesses and lighted only by a shaft of light piercing through a small window high up in the wall. At the far end of the room was a table with a number of bamboo chairs set about it: cheap Japanese lithography had been pasted to the wall, and garish posters that, advertising British commodities, had found their way over the passes with supplies.

The Depön was out walking when we arrived, although he was expected to return at any minute. In his stead we found the Rupön—a military rank signifying 'ruler of a detachment' or colonel—a kindly old man with a very attractive manner. He had recently returned from Calcutta where he had been to negotiate the purchase of two field guns and five hundred rifles on behalf of the Tibetan government, this force of arms being considered sufficient to keep the country secure from invasion from the north. On hearing that we had come from Calcutta he expressed the greatest interest and plied us with questions. First of all, how did we like living in the Underground Palace? He had been to the Underground Palace and, as the memory returned to him, launched into a long description of its marvels, a description which obviously lost much in the mouth of our interpreter, a Tibetan clerk from the Agency. For some time we were at a loss to determine the exact position of this house of wonder, until we realised that it was Fort William with its approach between two bastions to which he referred.

We were striving to explain that we did not live in the Underground Palace when the Depön entered. Having been warned of the arrival of strangers, and being under the impression that his visitor was McGovern, he walked into the room with a great show of coolness and dignity. On seeing us he broke into smiles of welcome and, having waved us to the chairs, clapped his hands for refreshments.

The Depön is about sixty years of age, and has an imposing figure, if inclined to be portly. His face is kindly, promising a sense of humour, and his general appearance indicates a man capable of bringing a shrewd judgment to bear upon the affairs of his province. He was frank and cheerful, and seemed to have none of the cunning often associated with Mongolians in his position. He made a short speech welcoming us to the Chumbi Valley and reminded us of the friendly relations that had been established between the Tibetan government and the British. Bishop having responded in suitable terms, the Depön gave a great sigh of relief at the termination of formalities, and settled down to the more genial task of entertaining us. A bottle of spirit was placed on the table and before each of us was set a small glass, exactly resembling the glass provided for water in a bird-cage and having the same stale film that collects inside a canary's glass when a change of water is long overdue. The glasses were filled from the bottle by one of the many attendants who had gathered together in the room.

The Eastern conception of an autocrat is essentially democratic; your true prince mingles with his people. Menials and peasants throng his room, showing the respect due to the father rather than the servility demanded by a tyrant. At Phari, Tchugro showed no more deference to the Dzongpön than he showed to the Bengali sweeper, but the impression of respect was not lacking.

The Depön drained his glass at a gulp and held it poised in the air until we had done likewise; then he returned the glass to the table with a slam and they were all filled again. The liquor was scented and sickly, a mixture of Eau de Cologne and petrol. Bishop managed to escape it by explaining that he was a doctor and was not allowed to consume spirits: to his mortification a cup of buttered tea was set before

GALING-KA

'*With its rickety bridge and straggling huts.*'

him in its place: on the whole the alcohol was the better alternative. The fact that Bishop was medically minded met with the approval of the Depön, who wagged his head backwards and forwards vigorously and was prepared to admit total abstention as a mode of behaviour proper to physicians; on the other hand he insisted that I was a soldier, and drinking being the aim and object of all soldiermen, drink I must. This plunge into military affairs brought a gleam of fervour into the eyes of the Rupön, who had retired from the conversation on the arrival of the Depön; he narrated the whole of the matter of the Underground Palace once again for the benefit of the Depön. My attempts to disclaim military rank failed; the Rupön brought irrefutable arguments to bear against them. First of all was I not obviously only seventeen years old seeing that my face was hairless: he had seen the whole of the British Army at Calcutta and they were all seventeen: and they were all the same height, a magnificent sight, rows of youths the same height and the same age, in short skirts. This description of the Cameron Highlanders, who were in the fort at the time, was received by the Depön with exclamations of wonder, and my own lack of skirt was attributed to the inconvenience of such a garment at great altitudes. In vain I protested, in vain Bishop attempted to come to the rescue by suggesting that I might be his disciple, a dreamer—he became almost romantic, but the Depön was adamant. I was too young to be a physician, and could only be a soldier: and so to rites peculiar to military men in their potations.

The Rupön drained his glass, leant over the table, and jerked it towards me with quick movements of the wrist until sip by sip my glass was emptied. And so, on the score of our common military ties, we engaged in a series of 'no heel taps,' to cries of *tashe dele*, the Tibetan for 'cheerioh.'

After some forty minutes of this, during which a second bottle was broached, he revised his estimate of my age and considered that I might possibly be twenty-three. Bishop with many grimaces attacked his second cup of tea, and the Depön continued to ejaculate chuckles and *tchas* in admiration of the vagaries of the British Army. The expected invitation to lunch followed, which we declined with a convincing show of regret, though we had difficulty in getting away. We presented scarves and took our leave. He escorted us to the door in a manner so friendly that the second bottle may not have been wasted on the score of British diplomacy, and at the final parting produced with great pride his one English expression 'Good-by-ee. Good luck.' To which we replied '*Tashe dele*.'

The ride back to Yatung along the river bank will long linger in my memory. There was a singing in my ears not unlike the chattering of sparrows on an early spring morning; had I been mounted on a brontosaurus I should not have cared. With three of those canary glasses poured down her gizzard I could have steered Rosinante herself to victory in the Viceroy's Cup. By the time we reached the Agency I was ready to eat anything, and the prospect of wielding a chopstick failed to raise a tremor of anxiety.

Eating with chopsticks for the first time is remarkably difficult; there is a temptation to move both sticks at the same time so that they cross scissor-wise over the object of the chase; also a bean or a chile, when attacked by a chopstick, is endowed with a special instinct forewarning it and at once becomes slippery, just as the limpet becomes endowed with a second sense and freezes to the rock, anticipating the fingers stretched out to pluck it off. Therefore, as in the case of limpets, it is better to fix an eye firmly on a bean at one end of the plate and pounce suddenly on some unsuspecting chile at the other: in this way a man may make a meal.

A kind of vermicelli, served up with meat and sauce in a round bowl, is an encouraging dish for a beginner; once connection has been established between the mouth and the bowl, with the aid of a little vigorous suction, eating vermicelli becomes a matter of routine.

The meat is made up into small elusive balls, and is served up with a great many side dishes containing various condiments, all difficult to negotiate. Once these are firmly gripped by the chopsticks they are dipped into a bowl containing sauce of the colour and consistency of blood. The novice will find, however, that they usually end by being deposited and not dipped in the blood, so that it is advisable to transfer them direct to the mouth if one is to make any sort of meal at all.

The food was washed down with *chang*, a light barley beer, extremely refreshing. The servants displayed a grave interest in our efforts and constantly replenished or changed the food before us, so that we should not lose patience in the face of continued resistance from one particular offender. McGovern proved to be an adept with chopsticks and made a prodigious meal; I must confess to using my fingers when some trite remark had sent all eyes another way.

After luncheon we played tennis, which proved to be amazingly difficult, not only on account of the *chang*, but because at an altitude of ten thousand feet any sudden and vigorous movement empties the human body of breath. A man who does not serve double faults may take an active interest in the first three points of his service game, provided his opponent does not return the ball. After the third time of striking he wishes to lie down and go to sleep, so that the chances of visitors to the Chumbi Valley giving a favourable impression of their tennis ability are remote. A series of gentle volleys from racket to racket is one solution of the problem and a game played in this style will sometimes last several minutes. We played on a hard earth court into which an iron framework had been sunk to mark the side and service lines. Mr. Macdonald, who was accustomed to the conditions, played a good game as soon as he had been placed with his back to the Trade Agency so that he could follow the movements of the game rather than watch the road to the Post Office for telegrams. But the pace was evidently hotter than we realised. He shed first his coat, then his waistcoat, then his watch: and finally leapt into the air with a howl before serving. And at that he won, for we had no breath even to cope with his initial service.

In the evening ten of us sat down to dinner at the rest-house, a meal consisting for the most part of a mixed grill made up of the contents of various tins in our food box; and so we celebrated the close of our short stay in the Chumbi Valley.

We had arranged to leave Tibet by the Dzalep La and to spend the night at Kapup, a hut two miles beyond the summit of the Pass. We proposed to leave Chumbi at nine o'clock and to take the march slowly and comfortably; McGovern with his caravan, which we had not inspected, was to assemble outside the bungalow at that hour.

At eight o'clock on the following morning Tchugro brought us the interesting information that the muleteer had disappeared and two of the mules were missing. We found the old mule and the miserable specimen munching odd patches of grass outside the bungalow, but no trace could be discovered of the other two or the muleteer. We realised that this little matter had been arranged in order to delay our departure until the muleteer had drained his full of the pleasures of his native country, whereupon Bishop rode down into the bazaar, whip in hand, unearthed the muleteer in a sorry and bedraggled condition and left him sorrier still. His defence was that the mules had broken loose during the preceding afternoon, had strayed down the valley, and, taken in the act of demolishing crops, had been impounded; it would be at least two days before they could be recovered.

After the previous effort to delay our march it seemed quite evident that this had been carefully managed: it was possible even that the muleteer himself had driven them down the valley and arranged for their detention. In any case it was essential to start that morning, for the loss of a day would mean a rearrangement of our plans, a double march, and great inconvenience. Fortunately we had only paid a deposit to the kazi in Gangtok who had hired out the mules to us, so that we had some hold over him.

We hired two mules from a head-man in Chumbi to carry our stores to Kalimpong for the sum of thirty rupees, paid him in cash, and deducted this amount from the bill due to the kazi at Gangtok. We considered that the balance of thirty rupees was rightly a matter that could be left to the kazi to settle with his muleteer when that worthy thought fit to return to Gangtok, so we ordered him to go up the valley, wait for the two mules and take them back to his master. Subsequently we heard that one mule found its way home alone, the other reached Gnatong and decided to stay there, and the muleteer, having thought the matter over carefully, considered it advisable to spend the rest of his days in his native land.

McGovern's caravan consisted of his servant Lhaten, who had been with him to Lhasa, a muleteer, two mules and a pack pony: the manuscripts that he had brought from Lhasa and Shigatse had been left behind at Gyantse, and arrangements had been made for them to be forwarded to him later.

Lhaten was a burly Sikkimese who had been born in Darjeeling; a good servant, with a facility for producing things from nowhere at a critical moment. He wore a rusty red woollen dress reaching below his knees, long woollen boots and a fur-lined cap with large ear-flaps turned back. He rode just behind us on one of the mules, who bore the name of Thunderbolt.

The muleteer took over the charge of our mules and the pack pony, a peculiar-looking beast in the last stages of collapse. He was the only survivor of the ponies with which McGovern set out for Lhasa, and that he survived was a miracle. His lean body had shrunk until it seemed the same size as his head: his mane was short and thick and only served to cover his ears: it did not reach to his neck, so that it gave him the appearance of a South Sea islander: his eye was wistful and human, with a curious cannibal longing as it rested on the nape of one's neck, which aided the illusion. His tail resembled a yak's, and stuck out straight behind him: he rejoiced in the name of Lhasa, and carried his master's great coat, which seemed to be too heavy for him. McGovern himself rode Punch, a Bhutia that had been sent to Chumbi to be trained and was on its way back to Kalimpong to take part in the Darjeeling races.

We left the rest-house at ten o'clock, having lost an hour on account of the negotiations for the two mules, and rode down the valley. At Piphithang we stopped to visit the headman. His house consisted of a large courtyard where we left the ponies, and an antechamber around which a gallery had been built, from which doors led off to the various compartments. The headman was away, but his wife showed us the temple, a small room containing a wooden shrine, elaborately carved with dragons and flowers. An attendant lama in the corner raised his eyes from his book as we entered, but resumed his meditations without taking further stock of his disturbers.

The usual number of retainers collected about us; men, women and children appeared in the passages; three girls, who were weaving on the gallery, stopped their work to smile at us, an alluring smile that sent a chill up McGovern's spine. It was a large house, altogether on a greater scale than the house of the Depön, for the headman was a wealthy merchant, trading chiefly in wool, and representative of the type of the Tibetan rich man, who makes his money purely from commerce, and not agriculture.

We rode on through Chumbi and bore southwards across the face of the gorge leading to the Nathu La, passing on our left a Buddhist shrine built on the banks of the Amo Chu. A mile or so further down the valley we came to Rinchenjong, an old Chinese village built at the foot of the defile that climbs steadily up to the Dzalep La, the highway for trade into Sikkim and India. The Chinese have long left Rinchenjong, and it is now a Tibetan village, similar to the other large villages of the valley, except that it is cosier and possibly dirtier, being snugly tucked up against the hillside and sheltered from the purifying winds that sweep up the valley. Here we took our leave of Chumbi and turned our ponies into the defile, which mounted upwards before us like a great ladder.

PIPHITHANG

'Wooden houses, with wooden roofs in the form of planks, kept from blowing off by large stones.'

IX

THE DZALEP LA

THE road to the foot of the Nathu La from Old Yatung, on the hilltop, rises so gradually that the climb is barely perceptible; from Rinchenjong to the summit of the Dzalep is one continuous ascent, and the existence of the Pass is impressed upon the senses from the moment one leaves the village. The stream tumbles down from it: the boulders are part of it, the close turf invites the traveller to linger for a moment in the sunshine before he leaves its beauty and faces the desolate and barren rungs at the top of the ladder: there is an eagerness in man and beast to push on higher towards the summit. Stone hovels in groups, roofless and gutted, blackened with the soot of the flames that devoured them, mark where the Chinese had their hamlets before they fled, or were slaughtered during the expulsion: a fairy defile, an approach to a fairy mountain: first sunshine and beauty, then the grim relics of adventurers who had lingered and lived in it: then bare trees and a wet sodden ground, and cold growing more perceptible at each turn.

The road climbed straight up in zigzags and winds through the blasted trees: then earth and rock, and more twists and turns at incredible angles, so that the ponies slipped and scrambled up each turn, and paused before facing the next ascent: and at each pause we turned and looked back down the path winding up to the Pass, and felt as if we stood on the pinnacle of the Temple. Some Tibetan women passed us bringing down bamboo fodder: a long train of mules wound down through stumps and gnarled branches that can never have been trees. We came to the snow line, passed through a large train of mules drawn up in a clearing, and reached the old Chinese rest-house of Langram, two miles from the summit of the Pass.

Langram is reputed in India to be a dâk bungalow, but the traveller who elected to make it a halt for the night would find himself in a sorry plight. The house has been deserted for the last twelve years, ever since the Chinese have been cut off from using this highway for bringing their goods to the Indian bazaars. For lack of ownership it has been transferred to the line of dâk bungalows in Tibet administered by the British Resident in Sikkim. A single-storeyed wooden building with two rooms and a short verandah, empty save for a couple of benches left behind by the Chinese, devoid of crockery or bedding: the windows broken. It would, however, give shelter to a traveller who had climbed thus far and found the Pass blocked, and is given the dignity of a dâk bungalow on this account.

The proprietor of the neighbouring Tibetan rest-house—a fat Chinaman, with a scanty peaked beard to his chin and merry twinkling eyes—acts as *chowkidar*. He had been warned of our approach and was on the look-out for us, so that he was able to stop us in front of his own establishment, tether our ponies to the railing in front, and invite us in. He conversed fluently with McGovern in a mixture of Tibetan and Chinese and took us across to the bungalow so that we could see for ourselves its unsuitability. We returned to his own house, which was warm and comfortable, and found two carpets spread out on two benches at right angles under the small window. Then he brought tea to us, not the Tibetan horror with its butter and grease: bad tea indeed, but made in a wholesome and civilised fashion, with real milk which must have been brought up from the valley in anticipation of our arrival.

We ate biscuits and chocolate and hard-boiled eggs from a basket that Lhaten had produced from his bosom. McGovern, seated cross-legged on his divan, told us much about his early life in China and Japan, and of an expedition he had made through Mongolia and Northern Tibet, and in this way we stayed much longer than we had expected. The ten minutes extended into an hour or more, until Lhaten became perturbed, and warned us that we should start at once if we wanted to be over the Pass that day, for bad weather was ahead. We found on going outside that he had cause for his anxiety, for the mist had mounted from the valley: it was cold and dreary, and the ponies were looking miserable enough in spite of their wraps. So, followed by salaams and good wishes from the *chowkidar*, we set out on the last stage.

From Langram to the top of the Pass the road is a succession of rungless ladders: we felt like bricklayers carrying hods up a lofty scaffolding. Lucifer led, and was tiring visibly: he stopped to breathe at each turn, and the fact that the ponies behind were forced to halt constantly in steep and slippery places wore them out to such an extent that we decided to drop behind: one rung in the ladder between each pony meant that we could at least stop at each twist in the path before scrambling up the next slope. The mist thickened and blotted out our surroundings; a cold sleet added to our discomfort.

The responsibility of bringing Punch through safely to his master at Kalimpong weighed upon McGovern who, in brown pointed fur cap and black poshteen, on a white pony with a red and blue carpet for saddle, presented a gorgeous picture of Robinson Crusoe at large in his desert island clothes.

The ladder ended and we found ourselves in a white barren waste, broken up by great masses of rock. Across this waste runs the single telegraph wire to India, and beneath it a narrow track showed up in the snow, winding through the desolate region of the Pass.

The mist thickened, so that I could barely distinguish the pony in front of me: the sleet fell monotonously, and a cold penetrating wind settled about us. The track through the Pass was about three-quarters of a mile in length, and we trudged along it in silence, nearly failing to notice the snow-covered cairn that marks the summit of the Dzalep La and the junction of India and Tibet. We looked back on Tibet, but fifty yards was the limit of our vision: only white mist, intense cold, and a strong wind blowing the sleet into our faces. We continued our march in a state of dreary discomfort, making neither sign nor sound until we had reached the edge of the Pass region, where we dismounted and started to lead our ponies down the steep descent towards Kapup.

The Pass is 14,400 feet high, and Kapup is 13,000 feet, so that the two miles descent is not nearly so steep as the climb from the

DZALEP LA

' A white barren waste, broken up by great masses of rock.'

Chumbi Valley. Instead of a scramble down bare mountain-side, or a slide down paths at perilous angles, we found long stretches of road made up of large slabs of stone, so that one can step downwards from stone to stone, as if descending a great staircase. The change from the climb and scramble of the morning came as a relief, and at the thought of the proximity of the bungalow and fire and food our spirits brightened up considerably. We had yet to learn that of all the varieties of road to be found in the Himalayas, the most wearying to the senses and trying to the nerves is the descent of a long continuous staircase of large slabs of stone, where every footstep has to be watched, where each pace forward becomes a jar on the body and a stab to the sole of the foot. During the hour's march to Kapup we had nothing but praise and affection for the road, and congratulation that we were descending rather than climbing; on the following day, when we spent over five hours in negotiating some nine] miles of this causeway during which we descended 6000 feet, we could find no curse, Eastern or Western, that could interpret our feelings.

The Kapup bungalow lies at the end of a frozen swamp at the head of the Kapup Valley, a narrow ravine some five miles long stretching from the foot of the Dzalep to the foot of the Nathu La. It is a white wooden building with a corrugated-iron roof, and consists of two rooms, each containing one bed. As a rule it is avoided by those travelling to and from Tibet on duty, for the usual custom is to make a long march from Chumbi to Gnatong; and should such an occasion arise we should prefer to follow that custom, even if every wind and snowflake in Asia were to howl about our ears.

By the time we reached the ravine the mist and sleet had turned into real snow, and soon after our arrival at the bungalow the snow-storm changed into a blizzard, so that we considered we had cause to bless the foresight that had erected a bungalow at the foot of the Pass: a further seven miles that day to Gnatong would have been a serious problem in view of the delay we had been caused at Chumbi and the time we had wasted at Langram; so did we reason, not having spent a night in that same bungalow of Kapup.

The night drew on soon after we reached the bungalow; the storm increased, and the wind howled up the valley. The walls were full of chinks and crevices through which the wind whistled: the floor had great gaps between the boards. With the blizzard came hail, which beat upon the iron roof with resounding crashes: there would be a lull, complete silence, and then such a crash that the Pass itself might well have fallen upon us. We turned in early and tossed for the beds: I got the floor, an advantage as I found later, although the draught that whistled about my ears rivalled in penetrating cold the wind that pierced the chinks in the wall. I first turned the table on its side and set it up against the door as a wind-screen; then I laid my Wolseley valise across the front of the hearth, pulled on every available garment over my pyjamas, put on a Balaclava helmet and thick woollen gloves, added glare glasses to keep the smoke out of my eyes and fell into a comfortable sleep, only waking on occasions when an extra squall beat upon the roof; then I would assure myself that Bishop was not suffocated before falling to sleep again. For of all the chimneys of this world that give forth smoke into a room rather than provide an outlet for it, the most efficient must be those same chimneys in the bungalow at Kapup under the Dzalep La. The room was full of a thick blue haze, through which coughs and splutters from Bishop rolled continuously. I opened the door into the adjoining room, but found that McGovern was enjoying a haze of his own of equal intensity; our one consolation was that the fuel consisted of good pine and not yak dung. And as the night drew on, the advantage of having lost the toss for beds became apparent; the hearth was raised some nine inches above the floor, so that the smoke, as it rolled out into the room, lifted slightly and cleared my head. I lay before the fire under a bank of smoke, comparatively immune from the fumes: my movements restricted but my breathing unhampered. Bishop, installed in comfort on a bedstead and mattress, caught the smoke breast-high and suffered accordingly; even when the fire had died the smoke still lingered, tossed about the room by blasts of wind.

The fumes of the early morning fire lit by Tchugro awakened us quickly enough. Snow lay thick round the bungalow, and opinion generally was against any form of ablution; to take a bath in the outhouse invited murder. I dressed on the flat of my back, and as I writhed there, struggling with a boot, my heart went out to the Tibetan for the filth of his body, and I loved him for it.

The morning was fine and clear, albeit the valley and the mountain-side were buried deep in snow. We took a last look at the Pass and then turned to climb the mountain-side opposite. The road was steep and narrow, but as a mule train had already passed along it, we had no difficulty in keeping to the track. At its narrowest we fell in with a large train proceeding towards the Pass, so that making room for it was a delicate operation. At length we found a shallow cave in the rock side into which we herded our own mules, and, by pulling our own ponies close against the mountain-side, left sufficient room for the approaching mules to squeeze past, which they did, with the usual jostlings and dashings and bumping of burdens.

The road rises to the Nim La, bends round and runs in a great sweep of barren rocky country to the Taku La, 13,300 feet, which frowns over the little valley at the bottom of which snuggles Gnatong; it was at the Taku La that the Tibetans built a wall and opposed the advance of the British in 1888. From here the road drops abruptly for one thousand feet. The sky, which had promised so well, gradually overclouded, and the descent was bleak and cheerless; the road was rough, consisting for the most part of large boulders and tracks cut out in the mountain side by streams. At the bottom of the valley we found a wooden bridge, strongly built and tarred, and beyond a small knoll the village of Gnatong.

Gnatong is an important village in Sikkim, being the first of any size on the highway from Tibet. During the expedition of 1904 it was converted into a large camp. The bungalow is good—a long wooden building built in the style of an Army hut with a parade ground in front of it. Here we stopped for lunch. While we were so engaged we heard a clatter of footsteps outside, and in marched a Gurkha corporal, with two privates, handcuffed to one of whom was a strange figure in Lama's robes. He at once threw himself into an attitude of extreme submission before McGovern, and shed copious tears. This creature turned out to be McGovern's secretary, who had played the rôle of master during the journey to Lhasa, and had been arrested for his misdemeanours immediately upon setting foot in Sikkim. As he had misbehaved himself during the Lhasa adventure, claiming among other things a bribe as a price for his silence at a critical moment, McGovern was content to see him punished. A long argument took place in Tibetan in which McGovern put forward his view logically but unemotionally, and Satan, for so he had been named, replied with considerable emotion if lack of logic. An appeal to us having failed, with groans and prayers the prisoner was led away in a state of collapse, his destination being Gangtok. Lhaten and the muleteer were in no easy frame of mind at the turn things had taken, although McGovern had assured Lhaten that no harm would come to him, whereas Satan would be none the worse for a spell in the jail on the hill at Enché.

We set out from Gnatong shortly after noon and passed through the village on our way to Sedonchen, where we were to rest that night. Beyond the village is a large mound on which stands an obelisk and several graves; this is the British cemetery, and the graves are those of the Englishmen who died during the Expedition in 1904, and earlier during the occupation of Gnatong by the Connaught Rangers in 1889 and 1890. There is an obelisk to their memory.

It is a lonely place, and the cemetery keeps a quiet vigil at this outpost of the north-east frontier of India: an impressive sight, those few crosses in the small enclosure, standing on the mound at the head of the valley, with the Taku La towering one thousand feet above it, and the Dzalep La barely seven miles away. A dreary desolate place indeed, with a wind that howls unceasingly; not a sign of tree or vegetation: only large boulders, drifts of snow, the squalid huts of the Sikkimese peasants, and the small house where the signallers keep an even more lonely vigil than the dead.

The road winds round the cemetery and climbs up the hillside. The valley closes in, vanishes: the road clears the crest, and there is a stretch of open country with a belt of trees, decrepit pines, the first sign of vegetation on this side of the Pass. The trees stand at the foot of a miniature mountain, and at this point the road divides. The right-hand branch winds round the face of the mountain at the level at which we then found ourselves, and seemed to be the easier and more obvious way; it was however *khud*, and of the earth earthy, crumbling, with a layer of frozen slippery ice—obviously unused. McGovern seemed to remember having gone by it six months previously and having found it practically impassable. He was, however, completely absorbed in the contemplation of a village which should have been where we were standing but was not, so we decided to take the other road. This led straight up the mountain, was obviously in use, and consisted of a causeway, carefully built into the side of the hill, and most excellent in every way. The only drawback was that it was not in our map, whereas the other road was: that we should have to go straight up the mountain—Mount Lingtu—and down the other side, a climb of 1000 feet, only to end up some three quarters of a mile from the point at which we were then standing, and at the same level.

The weather was getting worse, for a damp mist was creeping up, spelling rain and probably snow; however, inspired by the hope of finding McGovern's village at the top, we started up the left-hand road. The road, after the apologies for tracks we had endured ever since leaving the Chumbi Valley, was excellent, and the ponies stepped out with great vigour. McGovern followed behind on the mule surnamed Thunderbolt, since Punch had shown signs of going lame, and had been relegated to our mule train and the company of Lhasa, in the hope that he would recover before we delivered him at his destination.

We did not find McGovern's village at the summit—a peak, 12,613 feet high—but in its place were the remains of a fort which the Tibetans had built and held during their invasion of Sikkim in 1888. This invasion was a miserable affair, but interesting in that it represented the first direct clash of arms between Tibet and Great Britain. Alarmed by the secret exploration of their country by Surat Chandra Das and others, and informed by the Chinese that the British proposed to enter Tibet, substitute Christianity for Lamaism and appropriate their gold mines, the Lhasa authorities decided to invade Sikkim. They were confirmed in their resolution by the famous oracle of Ne-chung, who said that if they cared to build a fort round him he could by sleight of hand or other achievements of Black Art paralyse and destroy any troops that came against it.

They took him at his word, set out in martial array, and, climbing to the top of the first high mountain, built a fort and wall, and sat in it. To their amazement in course of time the Derbyshire Regiment appeared and chased them over the frontier by way of the Taku La, oracle and all. Had this success been carried further much might have come of it, but we deemed it wiser to shake our fists at them and return home: and the Younghusband Expedition became a necessity sixteen years later. The scene of the pursuit still boasts the name of the 'Derby Downs.'

The view from the top of Mount Lingtu, standing as it does away from the massive formation of the Donkhia Range, is reputed to be one of the most majestic in the world: unfortunately we could see nothing but swirling mist, and a gentle drizzle that was fast becoming rain, so that, having pointed out to McGovern the rural delights of his village, we were forced to descend again.

We scrambled down the path until we came to a small hut. This was situated at the point where the right-hand path rejoins the road we had taken, and was undoubtedly McGovern's village. In the hut we found Tchugro, the syces, and the sweeper, in company with Satan and his escort, taking shelter. They had come by the right-hand path and had had the greatest difficulty in getting through, the winter storms having washed great stretches of the path down into the valley. The sweeper's eyes glistened at the thought of the tales he was going to carry back to his *busti* in Bengal; and indeed many a torrid brow must have chilled at his narrative after his return.

This hut is an important post, for it marks the beginning of the great causeway that climbs down the face of Mount Lingtu into the valley of the Rungpo, a descent of ten thousand feet, six thousand of which it was to be our privilege to cover that afternoon—*Shaitan ko rasta* so called, 'Satan's Way,' appropriately it seemed, seeing that we had the gentleman, handcuffs and all, safely lodged in our caravan.

The monotony of that descent surpasses description. The causeway is a succession of large uneven slabs of rock: the sides of the mountain have been hacked and twisted by wind and rain into uncouth shapes and fissures: straggling rhododendron bushes add to the wildness of the aspect: the rain changed to hail, great hailstones that lashed against our faces and beat on our *topees*: a thunderstorm broke over us, sheet and fork lightning, and a crash of thunder that echoed among the mountains and rumbled in the valleys: a descent into Inferno that would have filled Blake with enthusiasm. Each step forward had to be watched, each stone picked out in turn—a long monotonous descent, where the senses become dulled and the brain numbed by the rhythmless shock to the body of each downward step, and by every lash of the storm.

Three hours passed in this way, hours of bewilderment and helplessness, with no change in scenery or sound, only a perpetual jolt down the face of the mountain. The path was converted into a stream, a cascade down which the rain poured to the valley; we were soon soaked to the skin.

At the end of three hours we saw a clearing, where the road opened out into a small plateau on the mountain side. A group of tall trees marked the beginning of the Sikkim forest, and in front of the trees stood a long log hut—the Sikkimese rest-house at Jeyluk: here we turned in for shelter and food.

The hut was divided into two: the first half consisting of barn or stable, where a few cows and ponies huddled together for shelter, woebegone and soaked by the storm. Beyond the stable was a small door leading into the rest-house, a low ill-lighted barn some sixty feet or more in length, occupied by platforms, now empty, upon which the muleteers are wont to stretch themselves and sleep in the approved fashion, each man removing his clothes and placing them over him as a coverlet.

There was a large stove in the middle presided over by a woman, the keeper of the house: by her side stood a small boy, clad only in a shirt—drying himself after some escapade—groping with his finger at the bottom of a tin that had once contained barley. He transferred the remaining grains one by one to his mouth with his finger, and grinned at us at first with startled admiration until, his shyness getting the better of him, he fled for refuge to his mother and buried his face in her bosom. She served us with a thin greasy liquid in a tin which went down well hot, but disagreed later with both Bishop and McGovern.

Our company was soon augmented by two arrivals, one a pleasant boor who smiled a welcome and ate his barley with much smacking of the lips: the other a man of such unexpected appearance that we all were startled. On his head he wore a black peaked hat: his thin straggling beard looked so typically French that we were amazed to hear him speak Sikkimese. Indeed, he needed but a portfolio to be a perfect picture of a French artist, of the Barbazon school: one of the 'Men of Thirty,' Diaz or Jules Dupré, either of whom could have done full justice to the scenery we had passed through during the last three hours.

We left him eating his barley, and set out on the last stage of the day's march. The road wound down the mountain side with the same monotonous regularity. We were now well into the Sikkimese forest:

the storm was over but the rain poured down steadily. We took nearly an hour to cover the last two miles to the bungalow, and found ourselves none the better for our rest at Jeyluk; Bishop slipped on one stone and pitched forward headlong down the path, shaking himself very badly. At length we came to an open green space, and found ourselves only four hundred feet above a cluster of houses and the bungalow, whereupon we burst into song, practically the only sounds we h·d uttered, except at Jeyluk, during the whole of the descent from the summit of Mount Lingtu.

It is said of a certain British soldier who, some twenty years earlier, carrying rifle and equipment, had formed one of a column of route marching up the road by which we had just descended, that he exclaimed that if Tibet was a bloody tableland, this was one of the bloody legs—a happy description.

The servants and ponies had pushed on to the bungalow while we were halted at Jeyluk. We found large fires and food awaiting us, and, when we had changed into pyjamas, life held out some object to us once more.

Sedonchen is a picturesque bungalow of two storeys, with large fireplaces, a verandah, and orchids in hanging baskets. The rooms were clean and comfortable, the *chowkidar* long skilled in supplying the wants of such as had swarmed down the 'leg' in a thunder-storm; and retrospect overcame our weariness and warmed our numbed brains. Bishop added to his reputation and our respect by dressing the cut finger of the *chowkidar's* small daughter, thereby receiving a large dish of fresh French beans by way of reward. Her finger was badly cut and she was very plucky about it, possibly not a little flattered by having a real live Doctor Sahib to dress it for her: her father, however, saw good to make up for the beans by charging us for four maunds, or three hundred and twenty-eight pounds, of fire-wood, alleged to have been consumed in two small grates in a space of five hours.

We turned in early and had a warm comfortable night at 6500 feet, in strong contrast to our disturbed slumbers on the previous night at Kapup, when the thermometer had fallen below zero.

X

SEDONCHEN TO PESHOKE

FROM Sedonchen onwards our march was to be through the pleasant valleys and over the hills of the Sikkimese forest: a switchback way, but warm: full of the beauty of trees and shrubs, wide rivers and bird and insect life. Of this way half was to be marched on foot, the ponies only being required for the hills. The roads throughout are excellent, level and metalled, and kept in good repair.

The morning was beautiful, following the storm, and the country side was a feast of colour. Armed with bamboos we continued the descent to the bottom of the valley of the Rungli. The causeway had stopped at Sedonchen and a broad road wound down the hillside through the forest. Occasionally we found a short cut and scrambled through the trees and down the steep face of the hill to a point in the road further down the valley. As we regained the road from one of these cuts we found our friend the corporal of police with Satan and escort awaiting us. He handed us a telegram that he had received that morning from Gangtok instructing him to arrest Lhaten, McGovern's bearer. McGovern was naturally perturbed at this, but there was no help for it but to give up Lhaten until we had got into touch with the authorities; so the wretched man was handcuffed to Satan and burst into tears at the indignity, weeping even more copiously when his dagger and money were taken away from him.

Our caravan by now presented a sufficiently formidable appearance, for the corporal agreed to keep with us as far as Rhenock, at which place he would turn northwards to Gangtok, and as the natives were under the impression that Bishop and I had arrested McGovern, we created more than a stir. In solemn state we continued to the river, which is crossed by a large stone bridge at the head of a narrow gorge. Here we mounted our ponies and McGovern his mule, and rode on a mile to Lingtam, a village with a large rest-house at the point where the road leads down to the level of river and winds along the bottom of the valley to Rongli.

We found a busy scene at Lingtam; a mule train was resting before the inn and the courtyard was littered with bales of wool and other stores; men were hurrying to and fro, and the sight of our caravan aroused no little interest. Satan and Lhaten were the heroes of the hour, and retired with their escort, our servants and a few friendly muleteers into the shelter of the inn to celebrate the occasion in liberal draughts of malwa.

Here we received the comforting news that owing to heavy landfalls in the valley during the storm on the previous day the road was completely blocked, that large stretches of it had fallen into the river and our only course of action was to return to Sedonchen and wait for it to be repaired. This announcement, while it explained the presence of the loads littering the courtyard, seemed to us to demand a certain amount of reconnaissance, and we decided to push on and see the damage for ourselves before accepting the advice so freely proffered. We called on Tchugro to follow and continued our journey in spite of the protests of the villagers.

We were now at an altitude of only 3,000 feet. The sheltered valleys of Sikkim are extremely hot, and we soon found ourselves marching in the full heat of the Indian summer: two days before we had been enjoying mid-winter conditions in the Tibetan passes.

The path descended rapidly to the river and resembled a bridle path through a great wood; trees shaded the path and served to keep off the heat, which scorched us in the open spaces. We came to the first landslide; the path was strewn with boulders and rubble, but we were able to lead our ponies over without much difficulty. We passed several landslides of this nature, all the result of the previous day's storm, until we came to a place where the path had been carried away sheer; a great slice of the hillside had crashed into the river, and to get the horses over seemed a problem.

While we were prospecting for a path, a band of coolies came up from Rongli to mend the road. Our servants also arrived with the mules, so that we succeeded with crowbars and picks in rolling sufficient boulders and stones to form some sort of track across the gap. We then unloaded the mules, led the ponies and mules over the boulders, hauled them up the other side, and then manhandled the packs across. Altogether we counted eight of these landslides, any of which would have made a sorry mess of us if we had been caught under them and two of which would have certainly hurled us all to destruction. On the whole we decided that the bogies had been more than kind in decreeing that we should descend the leg of the table during the storm, for if we had come a day earlier we should have had the gauntlet of eight landslides to run, and the chance of our coming through unscathed would have been remote; if we had stayed another day in the Chumbi Valley we should have had the task of crossing or attempting to cross the Pass while the storm was at its full height, and a night at the inhospitable bungalow at Langram might well have been the sequel. So we had no cause to climb the hill and seek the aid of a foghorn to appease the bogies, or press money into the good lamas' hands, unless by way of a thank-offering.

The valley opened up. We passed through a dirty straggling village, came to a wooden bridge across the river and found the clean comfortable bungalow of Rongli, which is as charming a place as one could hope to see. In front stretches the wooded valley of the Rongli river, with blue lines of mountains peering out of the haze; behind and above towers the wooded hill of Ári, our destination that night. The valley is open, quiet, and peaceful, and the great trees in it make mock of the heat shimmering over the grass: a scene combining the freshness and verdure of early spring with the blaze and heat of a June afternoon: two days' march from the summit of the Donkhia range and three days' journey from the plains of Bengal, a halfway house between the hottest and coldest of man's experience.

Orchids were hanging in baskets from the eaves of the bungalow: in front a trimmed grass plot with small flower beds, and a low red paling to which McGovern's mule, with a wistful eye on the flower beds, was tethered. This was the mule named Thunderbolt, and he proved to have a strong character and a mighty gift of song. He preferred to march one bend in the road behind the ponies, and ever and anon he lifted up his voice with the sound of a trumpet of brass. But this bray of his could not be forestalled, for he made it without effort, without movement of head or parting of jaws, so that the sound issued from apparent silence and one was at a loss to attribute it rightly to master or beast.

There is a tradition in the countryside that the water at Rongli is poisoned. We were unable to trace the origin of the story, but were warned of it by the servants, and McGovern also had been told of it when he passed through Rongli six months previously. The *chowkidar* was careful to insist that the water that he gave us had been boiled, but we did not put it to a practical test; the ponies, however, drank from a stream in the hillside and suffered no harm. Possibly in the history of the countryside is some tale of a village that perished in the night or of some siren that lured passing muleteers to their death; but the legend of the poisoned water remains.

Rongli is 2,700 feet high, and Ari, just over the summit of the hill that bears its name, is two thousand feet higher. The road separating them is good and winds up through the trees for four miles: going is steep but easy and the ponies climbed up steadily: Thunderbolt brayed frequently until he reached the summit, nor had we the heart to check him, for the placid calm of Rongli had gone to McGovern's head, and dragged from his lips such songs as no mule could face with equanimity. At the summit of the hill we missed McGovern, and turned back to search for him. We found him snatched from the jaws of death. Among the trees at the crest there are a few huts and into one of these Thunderbolt, without warning, had elected to go at the double. The eaves of the barn being breast high to a mounted man, McGovern's descent was swift and sure, and he was knocked off and dragged through the barn for some yards; fortunately he cleared himself from the stirrups and came to no hurt. As an omen we found three chortens just below the summit, with a convenient gap where a fourth might have been erected by the British Buddhists to the memory of their illustrious leader; but I could see no vultures at hand, nor had Bishop as much as a dissecting knife with him had occasion demanded its use.

The bungalow at Ari rejoices in a great bow-window, which overlooks the valley of Rungpo and the hill of Pedong beyond. The sky was reddening for sunset and across the opposite hill a great white cloud was creeping; a shaft of purple struck the cloud; the sky behind the hill toned to orange, then deepened to blood red: the cloud rolled by, and the colours gradually faded into night.

The hill of Pedong is British territory, forming the first buttress of British Bhutan, the strip of land between Bengal and the eastern half of the southern frontier of Sikkim.

McGovern sent a number of telegrams by his syce to the Rhenock Post Office at the bottom of the valley with the object of gaining Lhaten's release, and we turned in immediately after dinner. Bishop soon fell asleep, but I lay awake for some time listening to the servants whispering together on the verandah of the bungalow. A long monotonous drone proclaimed Tchugro in the middle of one of his interminable yarns, which swelled into a rumble as the narrative increased in excitement, so that I was moved to interrupt without disturbing Bishop in his slumbers. This I did by feigning to talk in my sleep, with great success, for the voice ceased and footsteps faded away one by one as the servants crept to their quarters. So peace reigned in the bungalow and I too attained Nirvana.

After breakfast on the following morning we took various photographs of our caravan. Lhasa the pony was, to our surprise, in fine fettle; he had fallen down four times on the previous afternoon when marching up the hill, and had refused all food except dry bamboo; he posed to the camera in excellent style.

We bounded down the hill to Rhenock, a large village with a post and telegraph office overlooking the Rungpo, the southern frontier of Sikkim, where McGovern found a telegram authorising him to bail out Lhaten for the sum of three hundred rupees, and did so, to the joy of Lhaten and the sorrow of Satan, who now saw himself consigned to utter darkness and, after a long supplication before the knees of McGovern, was led away by his grinning escort.

Lhaten, his cash and dagger restored, hastened with Tchugro and the syces to the local beerhouse, where he was rejoined by Satan and his Gurkhas as soon as we had passed from sight.

We took over our ponies from the syces and, after a brief halt in the village, which is large, hot and full of flies, rode down a path through shrubbery to the river. We found the main bridge broken down, but a *budli* of timber had been thrown across the stream a little lower down. Here we passed out of Sikkim, dismounted and placed our bamboos in tripod on a great rock. McGovern then having uttered solemn incantation we cast our bamboos into the sacred waters and turned our horses up the hill to Pedong.

Lucifer, perhaps to show his disapproval at thus rudely leaving Sikkim and Tibet, allowed Gyantse to take the lead up the hill unchallenged and dropped even behind Thunderbolt. This stirred Thunderbolt to action; having, as he thought, disposed of Lucifer, he advanced in merry mood to the heels of Gyantse. This led to a scramble and a rush, with Gyantse well ahead until we reached a narrow bend in the road, where the mule left the road and, contrary to the wishes and endeavours of his master, took the short cut across the perpendicular slope of the hillside. Thus he at last secured the lead, with a great bray of triumph, and held it until the road and country opened up sufficiently for the ponies to break into a canter and regain their own. We cantered into Pedong; a large village, compact, and seeming to be greater even than Gangtok. It was Sunday and market day: the villagers were thronging the bazaar and the place looked exceedingly busy. We showed our passports to a Police Patrol and rode up to the dâk bungalow.

The bungalow is under the control of the Public Works Department, and is provided for Inspectors and Forests men riding through on duty. It is excellently kept, with strong smells of varnished panelled rooms and good log-fires. Green curtains and a carpet in the bedrooms gave an atmosphere almost of luxury. But over it all was an impression of orderliness and the *raj*; there was none of the honeymoon charm and beauty of the Sikkimese bungalow, or the dirt, romance and buttery smell of the rest-house of Tibet.

RHENOCK

Large, hot, and full of flies.'

We found a hostile *chowkidar*, a scurvy fellow, who demanded our passes before unlocking the door, and would do nothing to help us. Fortunately the muleteer had left his companions to their carouse in the village—possibly he had some assignation in Pedong—and to our surprise drove in the mules an hour after our arrival, so that we could break open the food boxes, and lunch satisfactorily off potted meat, biscuits, brandy and the eggs we had in our haversacks.

The sky clouded over quickly and it became very bleak and cold, in spite of the fact that Pedong is only five thousand feet; rain soon followed, and we passed the afternoon in 'cut-throat' and song, tramping up and down to the strains of the catalectic version of 'John Brown's body lies a-mouldering in the grave.'

A few hundred yards below the bungalow was a large farm in the yard of which were a multitude of mules; these beasts were standing stock-still in the rain, their tails turned to the breeze, motionless, spectral: and yet close at hand was a large barn for shelter, devoid of mule. Not a tail switched nor hoof pawed: only a feeling of intense misery and discomfort: such is the nature of the brutes.

The servants arrived in the evening, in great form but presentable. The *chowkidar*, misinterpreting perhaps the cause of the singing with which we had beguiled the dreary hours of the afternoon, demanded in insulting terms exorbitant prices for a feeble fowl and a few eggs, and was surprised to find his fowl rejected and his conduct reprimanded with such energy that he fled to the safety of his own quarters. Even Tchugro, in whose throat malwa had left a kindly hiccough, had nothing to say in his defence. So we dined well off the remainder of our food tins and turned in at an early hour.

In the flickering light of the fire, the oiled wood panels of my room grew old and kindly, and I might well have been in some old English country-house: and with this pious meditation I fell asleep.

We were up very early and off early too. Our departure was enlivened by the chagrin of the *chowkidar* at receiving no reward save a note in the visitor's book as to his behaviour, and the efforts of McGovern to sell Lhasa to a neighbouring farmer for one hundred and fifty rupees; the bargain was not accepted and we rode out to Kalimpong without undue depression. As our party was to break up that afternoon we divided our baggage; for Bishop was to take Tchugro, the sweeper and the remainder of the stores by train that night to Siliguri: the syces were to ride Lucifer and Gyantse back to Gangtok, and McGovern and I, who were bound for Darjeeling, were to spend the night at Peshoke.

The road to Kalimpong lies just under the lee of a long ridge, through lanes and woods typical of any part of the south English countryside. We rode at a canter or trot, and while cantering I had the misfortune to drop my haversack containing camera and maps, which was never recovered, for we had returned to the domains of sophistication.

At one point in the road we had a magnificent view of the snows peering above a large white cloud bank.

We came to the famous Scottish Mission industrial homes, and while Bishop rode up to see Dr. Graham, McGovern and I pushed on to the town where we found an Oxford contemporary in the I.C.S. man, who gave us breakfast with most excellent coffee. Subsequently Bishop joined us and we went up to Dr. Graham's house for lunch.

Kalimpong is a beautiful place; it overlooks the valley of the Teesta, and is within easy reach of it: it has the hum, life and interest in the movement of things inseparable from a town on a great highway. Its houses are large and solid, and the men that live in them have a job of work to do and are bound up in their business; it is not a backwater, nor a refuge from heat of the plains, and in its energy and thrum has the advantage of its neighbour, Darjeeling.

Our lunch with Dr. Graham over, we felt that at length we had reached the end of our journey, and took the short cut down to the valley in no merry mood.

The road and trees, and gates, and dead leaves under our feet were so typical of England that Bengal and Calcutta seemed a far cry, an unreal nightmare that might hoot and grate but pass away into dreamless sleep. We clattered across the suspension bridge, took our last view of Teesta, and joined our caravan, which had assembled at the cross road leading to the railway station.

The pig-tailed syce, the black beaming sweeper, and two gaily dressed Darjeeling women holding the ponies, brought us back to reality, and bidding good-bye to Bishop, the servants, the ponies, even the miserable specimen of mule, McGovern and I turned our hired ponies to Peshoke, and bolted up the hill to the bungalow.

The interest of our journey had gone: Peshoke is beautiful, but it was off the highway, the way of contrasts; it had no pulse: it was restful, a place to smoke many pipes and dream many dreams: to drink in the beauty of the great woods and hills as the evening crept through them, or watch the sun gleam on the tea-bushes and change their tints before night enshrouded them in darkness.

So while McGovern argued his differences with the British Government, in the person of Major Bailey, I sat and discussed the modern generation with two Russian engineers, one of whom, an Austrian Pole, had fought against us in the war. That man can slough his skin in a generation seemed idle speculation; below us stretched a highway that joined men and beasts unchanged in a thousand years; what were international squabbles but smirches on the cowl of the ghost of man?

We talked until the differences had been settled in the bungalow, and then we all sat down to good mutton and ghost stories until past midnight; it was then that I heard the famous story of the Delhi princes.

We were off early on the following morning. The last miles to Darjeeling are fine enough, through tea-garden country and by a good broad road to Jalapahar and the barracks. My pony was a cracked, wheezing beast with an agonising trot; after his first spurt up the hill he seemed broken in wind and limb, and I was well pleased to see the last of him. And so we came to Darjeeling : a curious place: a humdrum mixture of modern and ancient horrors: a gimcrack town, inhabited by strange peoples with the languages of Babel: built up of tins and boxes and less planks than will keep out a draught: queer dirty lace curtains and notices of lodgings to let: constant badgerings of youths with ponies or donkeys to hire: red-roofed huts with fancy names, and a thick mist hanging before the great circular sweep of hill, blotting out all sight of hills or valley beyond: Clacton taken from its coast and planted in the foothills of the Himalayas: Torquay with perpetual fog over the bay: Government House, the clubs, and a great hotel full of Armenians and rich merchants; thrown in to give it dignity.

I slipped on my dinner jacket, snuffed the damp chill of the night mist and sighed for Champithang, Phari or Kapup; bugs, smoke, yak, smell, filth, brown earth, snow and cold notwithstanding.

In the early morning, on Observatory Hill, when all the ramshackle bunch of houses and streets is blotted out by the trees, Darjeeling comes into her own again. Right up in the sky from east to west stretches the unbounded range of the everlasting snows. Miles up in the sky, higher than clouds, in the glorious Himalayan morning before the mists have risen from the valleys: Kinchenjau in the east, and eastwards still the Donkhia range, and a hump with scoops each side, white and gleaming: and the scoops by the hump were the twin passes Nathu and Dzalep, by which we had entered and left Tibet: and from where I stood to the hump, and over the massive to Chumolaori beyond, winds the road to Tibet.

From Kalimpong to Phari: a way of beauty and ugliness; of hot valley and bleak mountain; of tumbling water and slow-melting snow; of pine-clad hills and bare treeless mountain side; of the song of mule-bells and the jingle of harness; a forbidding way to a forbidden land, with Lhasa far beyond all, city of romance, mystery and dirt.